unnoticed
NEIGHBORS

unnoticed
NEIGHBORS

a pilgrimage into the social justice story

ERINA K. LUDWIG

Copyright 2011
by The House Studio

ISBN 978-0-8341-2738-8

Cover Design by Arthur Cherry
Interior Design by Sharon Page

All Scripture quotations not otherwise designated are taken from the *Holy Bible, New International Version®*. NIV®. Copyright © 1973, 1978, 1984 by International Bible Society. Used by permission of Zondervan. All rights reserved.

Scripture quotations marked (*KJV*) are taken from the *Holy Bible, King James Version*.

Scripture quotations marked (*NLT*) are taken from the *Holy Bible, New Living Translation*, copyright © 1996. Used by permission of Tyndale House Publishers, Inc., Wheaton, IL 60189 USA. All rights reserved.

www.thehousestudio.com

This book is for everyone who made it possible—those both near and far.

Especially for Kendall.

CONTENTS

Prologue: Mud, Tears, and Redemption   8

 Plane Tickets, Jesus, and Aequitas   23

Paper Pearls and Grass Roots   43

Diamonds Are Forever   65

God Bless the Child   85

Reconstructed BB Guns and AK-47s   105

The Sick Need the Doctor   125

ABCs and TESOL   143

Sex, Slaves, and Sales   163

Gardeners and Greenhouses   181

Epilogue: A Compass, a Map, and Hope   200

Notes   211

"The greater number of us passes through this life with souls asleep. It is time we awaken from our long slumber and live with passion."

—CHRISTIAN PILGRIMS[1]

Prologue
MUD, TEARS, AND REDEMPTION

We are all pilgrims—every single one of us. Our earliest ancestors originated from dust and holy breath, but ever since we've appeared by some other mystery. We're born traveling, crossing one realm into another, to visit for a while. We arrive one day and grow and live, and stay for the interim, and then we're traveling again. Our journey is a long one—long, deep and wide—and it takes every bit of us. It is a journey not just on the outside, but on the inside too. It is a pilgrimage—a pilgrimage over, inside, into, and through life.

Pilgrimages are not new. They were journeys people took whether they were Buddhist, Jewish, or Muslim. Jews sought out the Western wall in Jerusalem to cry and weep and call for the Messiah, while Muslims made Hajj to Mecca to remember Muhammad and his prophecies. How the journeys happened may have been different, but the essence was the same, the point of them was the same—to go on a long journey or quest to a sacred place as an act of devotion and dedication. The word pilgrimage comes from the Old French, *peregrinage*, which in turn stems from the Latin word *peregrinus* (foreigner). The pilgrimage was something the pilgrim did, and the pilgrim wasn't from here.

I grew up Catholic. I was baptized, had my holy communion, became confirmed, did confession, went to Mass, and observed the liturgical calendar throughout the year. All the schools I went to were Catholic; in England, church schools are the next best thing to £30,000-a-year private schools. We celebrated Christmas, Lent, Easter, and Epiphany. We walked through the Bible through all the seasons of the year so much so that we knew which feast day meant it was the beginning of spring. One thing that always came up in the year was pilgrimage. Catholics like to journey. Maybe it's because Pope Boniface VIII declared pilgrimage necessary in the 1300s, or maybe it was because Jesus was always moving about—Galilee one week, Samaria the next.

My school had once been run by nuns. By the time I arrived they weren't in charge anymore and we girls didn't have to wear beige knee-length socks and brown shoes. But the nuns were still around. We saw them in the apple orchard or in chapel on our one-day-a-week visits to hear Mass. And we saw Sister Mairead with a coin box collecting money for the annual pilgrimage to Lourdes.

Going to Lourdes was quite the thing to do when I was growing up. In Lourdes the sick were wrapped in scarves and wool hats and rolled along in their wheelchairs, smiling into the camcorder held by a fellow traveler as they went to the spot where Mary is said to have appeared before a young shepherd girl. It is said that the water there is holy now and if you drink it or dip in it, some of that holiness will rub off on you and maybe God will have mercy and heal you.

I don't know how many people have been healed while at Lourdes, but I know that the hope of that place bound people together into a knot of compassion—parents with their disabled children who have never been able to speak, the blind held along by a friend or family member, the elderly whose backs have curved into a question mark but who still have the verve to hit back with a strong tongue. These and so many others visited the waters and the land hoping for a miracle, craving some justice.

In the fourth century, pilgrimages were hugely important for Christians. St. Jerome wrote several letters to the church in Britain encouraging all Anglo-Saxon Christians to go to Palestine to make progress in their religion.[2] He was hoping, on the eve of the fall of Rome, when people would have traveled on foot, by water, or on horseback, that they would take the longest and most dangerous journey of their lives. But it wasn't just that; he hoped that making that journey would strengthen their religion, their belief, their trust. And so they went. People left their communities to travel with strangers. We have Geoffrey Chaucer's masterful *Canterbury Tales* to try to imagine their conversations and entertainment. They stayed in monasteries and inns along the way and traveled for months, sometimes years if they were going to the Holy Land, for penance, healing, and revelation.

In the near dark ages, faith and God were more than ideas. They were so real people chased after them and even hoped to die near holy sites and relics to bring them closer to God. There's a reason why the Celtic church saw extreme value in a life of *peregrinatio pro amore Dei* (pilgrimage for the love of God).[3] Pilgrimages took people outside of their norms into something immediately more challenging and dynamic.

Maybe there's something for us here. Perhaps our lives have become so safe and predictable that we can walk through them blindfolded, knowing everything that's about to happen next. We're secure within our safety because it's familiar and trustworthy. We like our gentle faith and ideas because they are inoffensive and theologically sound. So maybe there's something to these pilgrimages, these times away that are meant to dare us into an adventurous and risky state of affairs, where we seek and ask hard questions and listen for the answers.

From time to time when I was a kid and had done all my homework and the weather was cooperative, my parents let me pitch up a tent in the backyard and sleep out under the stars. I had my sleeping bag, flashlight, wool pajamas, a sibling or friend and a faithful toy, and my entire imagination to run away with. I was an explorer, a scout. I was on an expedition, in the mountains, at the North or South Pole; I was outside in the wild. For me, there's always been something magical about sleeping outside. Maybe it's being so close to the earth that I dream of grass, or being scared and thrilled by the night sounds. Or maybe it's just being outside of the norms of my bedroom, the house, and the mundane.

Israel lived in tents. After Moses led them out of slavery in Egypt, they traveled into the desert in search of their promised land. For forty years they wandered in their temporary homes, falling in and out of faith with God. And so God gave them a festival to remember this time—*Sukkot*, which literally means "booth." In Leviticus, God commands that they have a massive celebration, with the best fruit and palm leaves and branches to wave and rejoice before God for seven days. "Live in booths for seven days: All native-born Israelites are to live in booths so your descendants will know that I had the Israelites live in booths when I brought them out of Egypt. I am the LORD your God" (Leviticus 23:42-43).

God orders Israel to take time off to have parties and remember the time when they were homeless wanderers. For most of us, being homeless would be an unimaginable nightmare. Not to live between brick mortar or panelled walls would be our undoing. And yet the Jews still call the holiday *Z'man Simchateinu*, which literally means "season of our rejoicing."

For many orthodox Jews, Sukkot is still a time to build tents outside. It's a time to make challah bread and other treats and eat meals together in those small tents and remember how their ancestors once ate manna and quail and began to imagine a free life. It's a time to remember a God who heard their cries and set about a massive operation to break them out, take them on a journey, and restore who they were.

* * *

For those of us who go on pilgrimages today, we usually start in the same place—asking ourselves, Why go? Why lose time, which is money, which we hope is security, which is insurance for the future? We go for the spiritual connection pilgrimage gives, for the chance to stand in those historical places, to put our faith in context and see its roots. We go to get some space and air to breathe, for clarity in decisions we need to make. But perhaps more pressing, we go because when we look around ourselves, we see things that make us think, make us question life at its core.

Our world is as beautiful as it is ugly. It's a contradiction and an oxymoron. There is mind-boggling beauty in its oceans, jungles, and deserts, and in the people and animals that inhabit it, but things are out of sync. There are plenty of resources in the world, but there is unbelievable poverty. There have been seemingly innumerable medical breakthroughs, but far too many of us die from preventable diseases. There are over 500 million Facebook users, but the lonely still exist. There are human rights laws that cover us all, but slavery and torture are still rife. The idea of equality is ingrained in our generation, but class, color, gender, age, belief, wealth, education, and background divide us and tell us we're all too different from one another. These realities lead to questions that reverberate around our heads until they're too loud to ignore. Even if we choose not to think about them, they remain, festering in the dark.

We're all aliens, but we're all human. We were made in his image on the sixth day, as the crown of creation. We were made in his likeness, and so our lives, our breath were to be honored and respected, safe from curses or murder. We were the last marvel of an intense and miraculous week of creating. We were made male and female to work alongside him in this Eden he had made. We were to be his representatives, to co-govern and care for all the animals and the very nature that surrounded us. And perhaps more so, to worship him through all of our actions.

Today, we're outside of Eden, and a lot has changed. We're still made in his image, we're still human, but our differences have become more pronounced. How we treat each other and this earth says we've forgotten the time in the garden and the order to be stewards together. And yet our insides are still the same. We feel joy, fear, love, loss, and hope. We all have that intrinsic instinct to want things to be better, stronger, brighter. We want things to go well for ourselves, our families, our friends. We want to be healthy, have work, be debt free, have a warm home and a safe future. In that regard, we're all absolutely the same. So, the issues in the world do not belong to the rest of the world; there isn't a "rest of the world"—there is only here. The world is here, and we're all pilgrims in it together.

My husband, Kendall, went on a pilgrimage once, sometime before we got married. He went in a group of nine guys to hike the Grand Canyon. They went for stillness and peace, camaraderie and the physical challenge—because when you trek forty-eight miles through arid land, you need some strength. He remembers the flight out to Vegas and the six-hour drive from there to the trail. He remembers the loops they took on the trail just to stop and see beauty around them. He recalls nights sat together, without a fire, talking about war, politics, and religion. He recalls the time they found Wrather Arch and stood underneath its aged and eroded arms. But most of all he remembers walking three miles in silence; he remembers his friends and fellow travelers Aram and Lawrence clapping for them when they reached the end of the miles. When I asked if they clapped because they managed not to talk, he told me "no." It had nothing to do with accomplishment. They clapped to tell the guys they were good, that this whole experience had been good, that they were loved by the God who created it all.

* * *

Pilgrimages are a lot like camping trips. They need us to plan, prepare, and think things through. They need us to start by asking, What should we take? Our packing lists fill up with the recommended clothing items, suggested tents, tools, the right footwear, and also a few luxuries. But a pilgrimage goes further than simply booking a plane ticket to Spain to hike Camino de Santiago to see St. James's shrine. The deepest journey happens in the secret parts of us, where the questions and hopeful answers meet. It's in our souls that we experience the searching and the curious interest. It's our hearts that need the honesty and resolve to keep pressing on, and most importantly, it's there where we need a pure openness to the unknown.

When we picture pilgrimages, we see people walking and hiking through valleys and mountain paths, trudging for miles to get to shrines or ruins. As a child my family went on summer vacations to the Republic of Ireland for seven years straight. My dad liked it because he said the green hills reminded him of eastern Uganda, and he would make us hike up them, just to breathe the air at the top. Of course, it didn't hurt that the Republic of Ireland is Catholic.

We would stay in cottages or bungalows and go for drives and walks until dinnertime. I remember wherever we drove there were always grottoes along the way. There would always be fresh flowers by saints' and Mary's feet or garlands around their heads, laid by those who had sent up prayers and questions. And I always wondered, Who built the grottoes? Were they leading somewhere? Did they take the people who were praying on a journey?

It's on pilgrimage that our souls begin the journey of being torn open and made vulnerable. It's where we go up mountain passes and come down transformed, like Francis of Assisi when he returned from Poggio Bustone to a life of dedicated poverty and meditation.[4] It's where we wrestle with the devil and our own wisdom to find truth. It's where we decide what we're going to do next with all of this compassion or understanding of what it means to be human, fail, and start over again.

The St. Francis of Assisi pilgrimage is a very popular one. Travelers can follow paths to show where he walked, stopped, prayed, meditated, and walked again. There are whole tours to commemorate the son of a wealthy merchant who renounced his riches to beg with the poor, fix the local church, and be disowned and beaten by his father.

Francis inspires us because he did the seemingly impossible. He had everything our money-driven era would want us to have and just walked away from it to hear God and hear people. And then there's the way he listened. He honestly took to heart Jesus's teachings of love and sacrifice, so much so that he didn't consider himself a brother of Christ if he wasn't cherishing those for whom Christ died.[5] For Francis, humanity was not just the result of creation but something he wanted. He wanted to be with others, he wanted to share life—both its peaks and troughs.

But Francis challenges us too. His oath to poverty goes against our grain. We know what poverty looks like—we watch the news and see people digging through garbage or rolling out mats in slums. We briefly see people in the neighborhoods we drive through really quickly in case they should approach us. Not Francis though. He got rid of everything besides the clothes he was wearing and walked barefoot with the poor, begging for bread.

At one point, Francis went to the Holy Land and met the sultan there, walked over hot coals, impressed the sultan, and allowed the Franciscan order to be the only Christian group to be permitted in Jerusalem. When he was there he walked through biblical sites and prayed and meditated. So many of us still do the same thing today when we fly out to Israel. Yet, Francis's pilgrimage was more than a year spent in the Middle

East; his entire life was a journey to find God and bring his heaven down to earth. It's really no wonder we go on tours to find where he walked and see what he saw. But I can't help but think if he wouldn't rather we took different paths and made our own pilgrimages and got revelations too.

This book is a pilgrimage of sorts. It seeks to go on the road, to taste and see what's around us. It's where I hope you'll meet lots of different people we share this world with. You'll meet women from northern Uganda who are AIDS and civil war survivors and Burmese refugees living down the street in U.S. neighborhoods. You'll meet those who go into caves to dig for jewels and others in suits who sit at tables and try to discuss fairness and peace on paper. You'll uncover why the poor remain poor, despite aid and charity. You'll meet boys and girls who call the streets home and those who camp out with them. You'll see the effects of small weapons on our dreams to defend and conquer. You'll hear the stories of sickness and healing and water's role in it. You'll see the saving grace of education and the real protection it gives to some from the most brutal injustices. You'll go behind and into the human trafficking underworld and return in the garden, where it all started.

The earth and so much in it is hurt. As humans we've both caused and suffered what's gone wrong. Whether it's war, human trafficking, children joining gangs in Midwestern states, flawed self-images that lead to eating disorders, or trade in minerals that makes only a few of us rich and impoverishes the rest, we've added to the problems, but we've also tried desperately to patch things up.

It's tempting to stand back, see the woes, and wait determinedly for a miracle to sweep through and fix it all. It's tempting to see Christ's sacrifice and bleeding display of love as all that's needed to change things, but I wonder if Jesus sees more for us. What if his words of "do to others what you would have them do to you" (Matthew 7:12) really meant we live the verb and love creation as he has and continues to?

What if things weren't left for governments to try to resolve or campaigners to fight but became our personal interest, our cross to bear? What if we stopped romanticizing poverty and all of its injustices by saying, "but look at how happy they are, even in all of that?" What if we wanted to see dignity—not just charity—in the lives of all humans?

People don't need empty pity. They don't need us to look their way once and push it down in a dark corner in our minds behind that dreaded to-do list. They need us to see they are worthy of living a life with self-respect and esteem.

We are not their saviors. We are their family. We were made out of the same mud and filled with the same breath. One writer was recently criticized for putting too much stock into the idea of the human family and for asking us to think like St. Francis and see each other as siblings—different on the outside, but siblings nevertheless.

We were all made equal until our ambitions, competition, and greed dug a divide that has pulled us further and further apart. But we have all been called sons and daughters of God. There are no nationality and citizenship differences, nor status restrictions, nor gender divides as far as God is concerned (see Galatians 3:26-28).

We all need saving, whether it's from fear, anxiety, arrogance, addictions, low-self esteem, guilt, or something else. We need to see that we have allowed or in some cases even created a separation between "them" and "us," what's "here" and my business and what's "over there." It's a separation that runs deep through history, and it's killing us.

But God's love is a big love and a redeeming one. He wants our hearts to swell and widen with that love so we can know what it means to be so rooted that we're not afraid of what we don't know and don't recognize—so we can embrace others and have plenty left over. So that life outside of Eden is more than just existence, but one to be savored and relished.

* * *

Ubuntu is an ancient African word that means "I am what I am because of who we all are." It's about community and others and how we're all each other. It tells us that it's impossible for a human to exist in isolation; we were made for company.[6] Individualism is the order of our day now, but it doesn't answer the craving in all of us for understanding and friendship. The first man needed someone, and that hasn't changed since. Being connected keeps us human and reminds us how every decision we make affects someone, even if we never see their face or learn their name. Paul says it well when he tells the Corinthians, "If one part suffers, every part suffers with it; if one part is honored, every part rejoices with it" (1 Corinthians 12:26).

Maybe when there's interdependence between us all, we'll care aggressively when there are hurts and problems in the world because it will be we who are hurting, not just someone else. When it's our family suffering we want to help, to kiss and bandage wounds and to love them.

Nelson Mandela shares a story about a traveler who is passing through a country and stops in a place for food and water. He doesn't even have to ask before the villagers serve and entertain him. But then Mandela says that Ubuntu isn't just about generosity. He says we're not wrong for wanting to enrich our lives, but the core question becomes: "are you going to do so in order to enable the community around you to be able to improve?"[7]

And I see that that becomes a question for us. A question to breathe into, walk through, and live out the answer. We're all pilgrims here. Maybe all we can do is try our hardest and hope those after us will do the same.

1
PLANE TICKETS, JESUS, *and* AEQUITAS

"May God bless you with a restless discomfort about easy answers, half-truths and superficial relationships, so that you may seek truth boldly and love deep within your heart."

—ST FRANCIS OF ASSISI[1]

Marsh Supermarket in downtown Indianapolis is probably the last place anyone would expect to be reminded of social justice, but that is exactly where I found it—in the checkout line to be specific. I was standing behind a woman who could have been Danish she reminded me so much of my brunette friend Sophia, when she stepped aside to pack her bags and revealed to all of us her beautiful African-American baby boy. He was standing up in the shopping cart laughing and playing peekaboo, and he had Down syndrome. His mother paid for her groceries, leaned in to kiss his round face, and slipped out the store doors.

Although none of us standing in the line so much as exchanged a word with each other, we all knew we had seen something delicate and overwhelmingly beautiful. Perhaps it was the baby's gummy smile or the fact that he had Down syndrome. Or perhaps it was just the way his mother loved him with that kiss and made him her own despite the controversy surrounding such an adoption that reminded us that there are needs all around us and when we love even one well, we do something lasting.

"Social justice" is a term that most of us have become very familiar with. We know it to be the organized efforts of individuals seeking to change and lift the hardships and challenges faced by others who are less able to do so for themselves for numerous reasons. Social justice hopes to bring clean running water where there isn't any. It hopes to raise money to buy enough mosquito nets to cap Africa's greatest killer, malaria, which claims more victims than HIV/AIDS. It hopes to free hundreds of children who have been stolen in the night and made to murder as child soldiers in Burma, Uganda, and so many other countries. It hopes to help train the next generation in the developing world with vocational skills so they can thrive in their communities and move away from dependency. Perhaps most simply put, social justice longs to bring hope, to let a hurting world know they have not been forgotten.

In September 2000, 189 world leaders tried to put social justice into practice by committing to the Millennium Development Goals (MDGs) to see poverty wiped out, to make the world a fairer place. They focused on eight different areas that are at the core of people's lives: poverty and hunger, education, gender equality, child health, maternal health, environmental sustainability, and global partnerships.[2] Their targets are both adventurous and noble and also incredibly necessary if we're ever to see change. More than one billion people in the world are hungry. Out of those numbers seven out of every ten of them are women and girls. And yet we send 25.9 million tons of food to landfills in the U.S. every year. That's the equivalent of $43 billion spent on food we don't eat.[3]

This isn't to say progress hasn't or isn't being made. Between 1990 and 2005, the number of people who earn less than $1.25 a day decreased from 1.8 billion to 1.4 billion.[4] So, four million people are a little better off now than they were before. It's hard to know whether to be glad there's been some improvement or rattled that we're still talking about millions and billions of people living in abject poverty.

In Malawi, the government and the UN set up a creative voucher program so farmers could plant seeds with the right fertilizers. The program was a lifesaver for them; for the first time in forever it made them food exporters rather than famine-stricken importers.[5]

I once volunteered in Uganda for a few months with a New Zealand-based organization that worked with local groups. I chose to be posted out in Mukono, a small but bustling town a little way outside of Kampala. I volunteered with a number of other foreigners from Belgium to Canada, and we all came with ideas of how we were going to save Africa. We read books in the lounge on the weekends when we were back in from the villages. We watched documentaries on a laptop when the electricity was working, and we wrote in our journals constantly.

And then one day one of the guys asked no one in particular why the locals don't just stop having so many children and fix the child poverty/orphan levels. I'm shy when I first meet people, so I doubt I said anything in return, but now I see what his question was asking. If the population numbers are lowered there will be less of a demand on already-failing systems.

But he didn't factor in human nature. We were created with the blessing and instruction to multiply and replenish the earth. We were born to continue the human story and the presence and job of guardian and stewardship. And children are the heirs. In Africa, children are insurance. They are their parents' hands and feet, legs and sight when their elders' all start to fail. They are their people's social workers and social security system; they are their retirement plan. And they are also the only way their villages, towns, and countries will survive into the next generation.

So maybe the UN's plan to prevent 350,000 women and young girls from dying because of complications during pregnancy and childbirth every year is protecting that insurance and future. Dying in childbirth sounds like a plot from a Victorian-era set novel, complete with the butcher instruments and late-arriving doctor. It's not something we're supposed to be worrying about years into the twenty-first century.

Then there is the big MDG target, the one that will change the rest of the other targets from aims to lasting realities—"global partnerships" or, simply put, trade. International relations is murky on the brightest days, and international development, the more scientific alternative to "social justice" can be just as complicated. Not because the needs aren't plain—they are. We see them in reports, in photographs, in testimonies, in current situations. No, it's because changing injustices affects us too. It asks moral questions on trading laws that act as an inverted Robin Hood tactic and leave the majority of the world on the fringes. And a truly fair international relationship would mean that developing countries would stop being called the third world and would simply be countries in the global community.

We read about and see social justice in magazines, in feature articles, in YouTube videos, at festivals and concerts, and of course all over the Internet. In April of 2010, the *Guardian* newspaper in London launched a huge social-justice-themed article competition focusing on the needs in Africa and Asia.[6] The social justice movement has become so popular in this new millennium that it has inadvertently contributed to the ever-increasing promotional t-shirt production industry.

Yet before the term social justice became so widely known and so imperative, it was rooted in a Latin word and Roman mythology. *Aequitas* means justice, equality, conformity, symmetry, and fairness. It is from where our word "equity" is derived. Aequitas was also a minor Roman goddess who represented fair trade and honest merchants. Pictures of her holding a scale to depict the balance of fairness and equity have been found on ancient Roman coins. Perhaps for most of us today justice still means the same thing—fair opportunities for everyone regardless of who they are, where they are from, or what they look like.

In 1999 in the U.S. alone, there were a reported 1,202,573 non-profit organizations. By 2009 that number had leapt to 1,581,111 non-profit organizations.[7] These organizations were and are everywhere—but particularly at music festivals. Summer music fests are a staple of American and British life. They mark the beginning of summer, vacations, heat waves, freedom from work and school, campfires around which to talk about deep and meaningful things, and of course romances.

One of the least likely romances has been between humanity; yet there it is on the thousands of fliers copied at Kinko's. It's on the girl wearing the bright purple ribbon strapped around her forehead which reads "love" in paint. It's at the booths where a guy is selling woven Peruvian satchels to send the money back to the community he met last Easter. Something has happened to us, and it runs deep in our veins and in our breath. Maybe it's the revival that is preached so often, or maybe it's a slowing down and taking stock of things. Maybe we're opening our eyes and seeing with mercy what living in faraway lands looks like and have seen that what is happening there is meshed up with what is happening here.

It is difficult to pinpoint exactly when social movements and organizations swelled onto our social scenes. The founders behind Invisible Children are probably some of the better-known ones. They brought the plight of Northern Ugandans into American homes with their home-video camera documentary that collected the lives and names of those suffering under the Lord's Resistance Army.[8] A mere eight years later, the organization now has teams in colleges and schools across the country with scores of children, teens, and young adults saying the same thing: "What can I do to help?"

It's that one simple question that delves into the core of social justice. It is not merely reading the news of national and international tragedies and thinking detachedly as Bob Geldof's 1980s hit song "Feed the World" eloquently put it: "Well, tonight, thank God, it's them instead of you."[9] Instead, social justice invites us to partake in the messy affair of human life, both in its horror and beauty. It asks us to examine our own lives, to see beyond the borders of our neighborhood lines or far-reaching geographical and linguistic differences to see what we all have in common—humanity.

There is a couple in Nashville, Tennessee, who opened a thrift store nearly two years ago with the simple desire to give proceeds to refugee children in the area so they could buy new school uniforms or have dresses for their proms. When I asked them why they called their store Humankind they replied, "The name Humankind simply refers to the fact that we are all human—part of the human race, with all the same basic needs, one of those needs being clothing."[10]

It started with Christina teaching a third grade class at one of Nashville's metro public schools for a year and noticing one little Somali boy. He was the smallest boy in the class with one of the longest names—Abdirahmani. Every Monday he would come to school in his clean, freshly pressed yellow button-down dress shirt that was too big and wear it every day until it could be washed and ironed over the weekend. It wasn't that his family was lazy or neglectful but that he didn't have enough school-appropriate shirts. Abdirahmani wasn't the only one in need in a class where half the students were Somali or Sudanese refugees—in need not only of a school uniform but of the confidence and normality clean clothes can give.

Nashville, Tennessee, has many refugees. They're from Iraq, Iran, Somalia, Sudan, Myanmar (Burma), and other places. They hope for a peaceful life where they can work, learn, and rest in safety without the fear that hounded them before. They live where we don't see them until Nashville Public Television shows a special on "next door neighbors"[11] and we learn how many had become new citizens.

Nashville isn't the only city where people live in bubbles. We all do; we just don't know it. Imagine having neighbors you didn't know existed. Imagine living in a city where the lines are so neatly drawn you don't notice that you've never met anyone Kurdish because there aren't any Kurds anywhere around you. They don't go to the same grocery store, or the same doctor, or bank, or park.

When I lived in Nashville, I ran a project for a while called "My Name is . . ." I had met some refugees and new immigrants and they were interesting; their stories were rich and their hospitality was even better. And I wondered why my colleagues didn't know that not far from where we worked there was an Iraqi family in which the mom made the best sweet date pastries. It was a project about making real introductions between refugee communities and their American neighbors. It said hello with the words of Iraqi and Burmese children and with their colorful hand drawn pictures. They gave stories of school lunches, their families and best friends, their favorite toys and hobbies—all those things that are important when you're nine years old.

When we talk about humanity and its needs and the fight to see justice being done, we sometimes forget these topics are not new. In the Old Testament, God commanded Israel: "Administer true justice; show mercy and compassion to one another. Do not oppress the widow or the fatherless, the alien or the poor" (Zechariah 7:9-10). Numerous times throughout the Bible, God goes on to remind Israel, and in turn, us, to *protect* the vulnerable—not exploit or ignore them.

Jesus took the plea further and summarized the majority of his whole ministry in his most famous teaching: "A new command I give you: Love one another. As I have loved you, so you must love one another" (John 13:34). Or, "Love your neighbor as yourself" (Mark 12:31). From the Beatitudes to overturning the tables of the money changers in the Temple, Jesus made his stance on fairness very explicit. His response to the hunger of a crowd of 5,000 was just as compassionate and as active as when he wept outside the tomb of his good friend, Lazarus.

Jesus cared about people in such a burning and unceremonious way that it shocked countless people, riled his critics, and earned him flocks of admirers to his sermons. And yet one thing that it so spectacularly wonderful about the way the gospels are written is that it is not just the fantastical large events that are reported but the smaller, more awkward ones too.

When Jesus met a Gentile woman in the Tyre and Sidon region, his first response to her request for help for her daughter was silence. Utter silence. Jesus kept so quiet while the woman continued to ask for help that his disciples insisted he send her off to stop her begging (see Matthew 15:21-28). Then when Jesus did finally speak it was only to remind her he first had to help the sheep—Israel. It is as though Jesus was reaffirming all the racial prejudices of the day between the Jews and Gentiles, something that would definitely have led to a lawsuit today. And yet this woman who was fighting for her daughter's life to be spared was undeterred. She replied to his statement with wit and humility and earned acclaim from him: "'Dear woman,' Jesus said to her, 'your faith is great. Your request is granted'" (Matthew 15:28, *NLT*).

When I first read this story I was mortified and confused at Jesus' approach to the woman's suffering. It was only with time that I was able to peel the story back to see how God was challenging all of our hidden superiority complexes and drawing us back to the fact we are to have compassion and mercy despite what our histories and cultural differences may suggest.

In September of 2006 I took God's mandate to care for the downtrodden quite literally and spent my savings on a plane ticket, sold my extensive collection of clothes and jewelry, and worked two jobs in order to fund a volunteer position in Naggalama, a tiny Ugandan village. I was adamant that I wanted to give back to others at least some of what I had received. Some may say it was the age old Western guilt that motivated me or my naïve Christian ideals that launched me into the overcrowded classroom that served ages four to twelve, but I think that simplifies it too much.

Naggalama has one hospital and it's barely equipped. The walls were a pale yellow, and the floor was plain, worn concrete. It was my first week there—I had arrived a week too early, so I was following the local community center staff around and trying to get my bearings. On one of those days, while a man named Samuel took me on a tour of the hospital, a woman and her friend rushed in with a bundle in their arms. I couldn't see what it was at first because it was wrapped in a *chetenge* (an African print sarong-type fabric). Then the package was unwrapped and I saw the frailest set of limbs fall on to the bed. The doctor later translated for me that the women had walked miles to bring the little girl there. She had malaria, and she was dying. It was my second day on my placement, and I was watching a child die. I know it's cowardly, but I wanted to go home in that moment. I suddenly understood and could see what working for social justice would mean, and I didn't want it.

When you see children in sweating malaria fevers, or school houses that were being built but have been left unfinished because the funding has run out, when you see people staring at you unexpectedly because you're just another foreigner who's come to help for a bit and then leave, you start to wonder what you have to give. How could you possibly understand what it means to wake up before the rooster cries to collect firewood for the stove and collect a few vegetables for lunch as that's the only meal you and your family will be eating? Or what it means to walk miles, literally, to fill up a yellow jerry can and carry it back miles, even though it's nearly the same height as you? Or what it means for this to be your life every day without even the slightest chance of something different?

I would have given up if it weren't for a stranger in the village who quizzed me about whether Tony Blair, the British Prime Minister at the time, or maybe the UN, had paid for my plane ticket to come over. Upon realizing I did this voluntarily without any sponsorship or funding, the stranger stopped, looked at me closely, and said, "Thank you for remembering us."

* * *

It is easy to picture DEET sprays, mosquito nets, and volunteering in Uganda. The news reports, award-winning photographs, and anthologies have given us eyes to see those troubles. There's something profound about poverty so severe and being part of the solution. But possibly a few miles from where we all sit, there is another kind of justice happening.

David Gould and his family of five pastor and love the challenged, low-income community at the intersection of Nashville's South 6th Street and Shelby Avenue. Every week they open their doors, kitchen, and quite possibly their sanity to a motley of people who are fighting off and caving in—to drugs, violence, abuse, and a poverty that is peppered across America. They offer food, basic home and personal goods, a chance to talk about the week but perhaps more importantly, recognition.

The Goulds know people's names. They know where they live and how their children are doing in school. They ask about those family relatives and that landlord. They don't miss a beat. In the summer they hold services in the parking lot and worship with these neighbors. They hold them and pray with them when they come forward and sing the songs they know over and with them. They dish out hot dogs and chips or spaghetti. They give out sweet tea and water to lessen the burning heat.

And they listen to them and encourage them with a simple, old message: "Don't give up."

Social justice is the old concept that has found a new home in this much smaller world we live in. The Internet, WiFi, Facebook, Twitter, Skype, and twenty-four-hour news mean information and ways to contact are all around us. Distance is barely an obstacle anymore; everything is closer. We know when there's a revolution and a mudslide and people are left without homes or protection. We know when one country fires at another or leaves people displaced in their own lands. We know when something goes wrong at a rig and oil just keeps spilling across the ocean and devastates marine life. We know when guns, drugs, and violence escalate on our street and leave scores of teens dead.

If technology has brought us close to what is happening to each other in real time, recent economic struggles have woven us even more tightly. The 2008 economic crisis saw banks collapsed, homes lost, jobs taken, and an international spending slump—the worst we'd seen in years. For the last couple of years everyone has been trying to restore the economy and our trust as we now face spending cuts, unemployment, high rent and taxes, and rising food and fuel prices.

If we were concerned for the poor in the past, we're now having to be concerned about running our own homes against rising costs, finding work when there barely is any, and trying to reconcile this new era where our money, governments, and business leaders are fragile. And yet, it's now that we have to scour our hearts and see that we're all in this together, some worse than others, but we all need each other. Charities and not-for-profits still need us to be outraged by the greed of some that has imprisoned and punished others into generations of poverty. They still need us to be indignant and resilient about wanting justice served fairly for all. And those on the edge need us to remember and fight with and for them.

Micah and his prophecies fill up only a small book toward the end of the Old Testament, but their message is loud. Micah sounds like a sensitive soul, worried about what was happening in the small towns and villages that neighbored him. He speaks of hope, and he speaks of doom—the common extremes of his time. But then he lists questions about what God wants from us in all of this, from sacrifices of rams to ten thousand rivers of oil (see Micah 6:7). He settles on one plain and resounding answer: "To act justly and to love mercy and to walk humbly with your God" (Micah 6:8).

We still need to show mercy and seek fairness. We still need to see the needs of others, see them as more than our own. That is when hope becomes more than an idea and justice becomes true, genuine love for people. And it's not that we're being asked to do this on our own; we've been given an example that was in flesh and blood. And we've been promised his company as we try to live this out. But maybe living it out will demand more than we think because it all has to start *in* us before we can see it *out* there.

Making the rights journey

Human rights are broken. You've done the reading, watched the documentaries, heard the stories, seen the evidence. Now what?

Join Amnesty International in taking practical steps toward undoing the unfairness that surrounds us. Register with the Rights Journey and sign petitions, participate in a discussion forum, join a "virtual" event, and add your efforts to teams of others to help bring about change.

Use your voice. Start here:
http://www.amnesty.org/en/rightsjourney

Dinner talk

There's a ton of information out there and online about the injustices around us; keeping it all to yourself could bring on the onset of spontaneous human combustion.

Why not organize a dinner, invite some friends over, and quiz them on their knowledge on the world's hunger, trade, and health issues?

Don't just show off—educate.

Information upload

Reading = quest for knowledge and understanding.

Broaden your horizons and read as much as you can about social justice issues. It may just give you something highly witty and intelligent to add to the conversation that's been going on for years.

Not sure where to start? Follow the dots . . .
http://www.librarything.com/tag/social+justice

Traveling sisterhood pants

According to the UN, women and girls are the most likely to go without education or opportunities. They'll also be the ones collecting the water, working the subsistence farms, feeding the livestock, and getting the daily meal ready—all before everyone else wakes up.

Women in the U.S. also face their own struggles. On September 15, 2010, 70,648 women were receiving medical treatment as victims of domestic violence. Domestic violence hotlines received 22,292 calls.

Show your support by seeking out a women's shelter in your area and taking them your used, but good, clothes, shoes, and accessories.

Go to http://www.nnedv.org/resources/census.html for more information.

Let's party, baby

Okay, I know you thought I was going to say put on your kitten heels or that sleek vintage vest you just found at Goodwill, but how about throwing a party for all the babies born in poverty without the basics?

Every year, 536,000 women and girls die as a result of complications during pregnancy, childbirth, or the six weeks following delivery. Ninety-nine percent of them occur in developing countries.

Every year, more than 1 million children are left motherless. Children who have lost their mothers are up to 10 times more likely to die prematurely than those who have not.

Throw a baby shower, bake (or buy) a cake, invite your friends who have tons of baby onesies that they've been desperate to get rid of and send them off with a card and lots of love.

Go to http://www.maternityworldwide.org/pages/alternative-gifts.html to learn how to send off your gifts.

Buzz off

Africa's biggest killer isn't AIDS; it comes from those little parasites that make a drill sound right by your head when you're trying to sleep.

Malaria kills a child in the world every 45 seconds.

Close to 90 percent of malaria deaths occur in Africa, where malaria accounts for a fifth of childhood mortality.

There were an estimated 243 million cases of malaria in 2008, causing 863,000 deaths, 89 percent of them in Africa.

$10 will buy an insecticide treated net, and pay for distribution and education on prevention.

$10 will save lives. That's humane economics.

Send a net to sub-Saharan Africa with:
http://www.nothingbutnets.net/nets-save-lives/

Pantry wonders

The local church is a catalyst out there. It's the community center, refuge, hideout, second home, only home, childcare, counseling center—the saving grace to so many.

In India, it fights for the *dalits* or "untouchables."

In Camden Town, London, it gives the homeless a place to sleep safe from London's cold streets.

In Indianapolis, it's the comfort to the woman who recently divorced and is trying to work out what life is like with just the kids.

Most churches have a volunteer sign-up program. Put your name down, give a little time, see what love feels like.

2
PAPER PEARLS
and
GRASS ROOTS

"Father, forgive them; for they know not what they do."

LUKE 23:34, KJV

We've heard these words before and perhaps even seen dramatizations of this death scene in films both reverent and critical. It's been quoted in poetry and prose; yet, it's very unlikely many of us can truly fathom the depths of it. Forgiveness is something we're encouraged to do, to avoid grudges that turn into ulcers, to keep our sanity, and most noble of all—to be better human beings. Theoretically, forgiveness sounds and seems doable, but then we start to grade it depending on what it is we're being asked to forgive.

After traveling to Kitgum, in northern Uganda, a few years ago, I realized forgiveness has never been so clearly illustrated this side of the cross as it is there. For decades Uganda has endured civil unrest, kidnappings, brutal killings, torture and forced recruitment of children into the Lord's Resistance Army (LRA). The story of LRA, child soldiers, and the pillaging of northern Uganda is as weird as it is tragic. A young woman named Alice Lakwena was from the Acholi tribe in the northern most tip of the country. She was a traditional spiritualist, but she also read the Bible. She started to believe that the Holy Spirit had told her the Acholi people were supposed to govern Uganda and that they would if they fought the Ugandan army with nothing but basic weapons and oil on their skin, which would protect them from bullets.

It sounds like a warped fairytale, but when her relative Joseph Kony took over her position in the community and pushed for civil unrest, Uganda entered a war that still mars people's psyches today. Children were kidnapped in night raids and forced to turn around on the spot and kill their own parents and family or else be killed. When children are forced to kill to push forward a strange spiritual-political ideal, they've become mere pawns, and the hurt goes deep because children are the insurance, children are the tomorrow.

Murder was never meant to be part of this world; death was never meant to enter it. When Cain tricked Abel and killed him in a field, something in humanity broke. Yes, their parents had already disobeyed, but they had left blood alone, the life that's in us. Genesis talks about Abel's blood crying out from the soil to be seen and noticed and given justice. God hears and exiles Cain, but he still protects him. Murder tore the first family apart and though it's not written, I think it tore Cain inside too.

Invisible Children grabbed America's attention with their off-the-wall handheld camera documentary about the night-commuting children who walked miles to sleep on the verandas of hospitals, schools, and bus parks to hide from the dark world of the rebel war. And, for the women—the mothers, sisters and daughters—who survived, their story continues.

Esther Akongo sat on a thatched stool near the Cornerstone guesthouse when she told me how after her husband died from tuberculosis in 2002 and how in 2003 the Lord's Resistance Army (LRA) in Kitgum abducted her and her eighteen-year-old son. She was calm and collected when she recalled how the rebels then killed her son and demanded, if she was Jesus, she raise him from the dead. They left her in the forest with him, and she made a stretcher from twigs and thick leaves to drag him along so she could bury him back in their village. She didn't cry when she told me this story—perhaps she spent all her tears when left alone with her son's body. But even more confounding is that she has no malice for the pubescent killers and instead insists: "They're our children; they're Acholi. They didn't apply to be rebels. They were abducted."[1]

The Acholi people have a way of forgiving and cementing reconciliation. It's a traditional custom and one that has been passed on orally. Whoever commits a crime is given a bitter drink mixed with herbs and water and made to step on a fresh egg. The sour drink and egg mark the end of the past. A line has been drawn under it. It is left in the past. The son or daughter is now in the family again. For a former child soldier this is the difference between rebirth and an expected life of exile.

Rose Ochoa is an impressively tall, strong woman—one who would surely win an arm wrestling contest. But her spirit is gentle and so full of the persevering patience that can be found all over northern Uganda that it draws you into the work she has done to see these widows become self-sufficient citizens again. With fishing wire, unwanted colored calendar pages, glue, scissors, pencils, and rulers, Rose has been able to teach ladies how to create beads that can be turned into bracelets, necklaces, or earrings. She then buys them from the women and sells them in Kampala, Jinja, and Mbale.

A group of women in Buvunya, a very small village somewhere near Jinja, started their paper pearl collective with Rose. In their first training session, they sit in a circle around a table in one of the lady's houses and watch carefully as old poster paper is rolled into a bead. They chatter as they feed the beads on to the fishing wire and coat them with wood varnish and hang them in the sun to dry. They smile as they sort the different colored beads into groups. They grin and laugh, delighted as they add clasps and earring hooks to the jewelry they've just made. You would never know that AIDS has taken a few of their husbands or that the country's poor economy gives them only 3,000 Ugandan shillings a day.[2] You see only a pride that they're working and making a product that can help them pay their children's school fees and buy another goat or some more chickens.

Sometimes I wonder if this steely resilience is what some people use to dismiss the extent of the hardship here—to say that these people have adapted to the hardship and we should just let them get on with it. But hardship was never supposed to be the norm for anyone. The ground used to water itself before the first rains came. Adam tilled the garden with relative ease and enjoyed its produce, but the curse changed everything so completely. God's words when he exiled Adam and Eve meant that we would eat only by sweat and painful toil. Instead of lush green vegetables and plants, we would get thorns and thistles. To Cain, his words were even harsher.

It was my friend and fellow volunteer, Malcolm, who took me out to join him and Rose in Buvunya. He did it because he was setting up a website called "Grassroots Uganda" to help sell their eco-friendly jewelry online to a much bigger market. He started with the women collectives in Uganda and then did the same thing in the Philippines. The women make the products that he helps sell via PayPal, and they receive 100 percent of profits for their small businesses.

Malcolm is a good guy. He was leader of our volunteer pack, though he would never admit it. He was the kind one and the one with the strong Kiwi (New Zealander) accent. He is also the most Christ-like atheist I know. Malcolm and I spoke a lot about God in suffering and God in pain. We picked through the Bible and wrestled with its meaning and its relevance today. We settled on getting to know these villagers and serving and helping them any way we could—Malcolm by running the website writing short biographies to give people a chance to have a glimpse into these often, truly isolated communities, me by collecting their stories and telling them over and over so that they're never lost or forgotten.

I like to think if Jesus were around in flesh and blood today he would build a website. He would build it out of his own pocket too and take pictures of these women smiling or looking grave (Ugandans like to look very stern in photographs). He would upload their photos and write down their stories. He would listen as they talked to him, and he would tell them he's sorry that they've suffered and he knows that doesn't make everything all better. He would tell them those nights they prayed, he heard, and he was there.

* * *

Indianapolis has the largest Burmese refugee community throughout U.S. cities. Most have fled the war and the persecution under the military government. Most have given up their homes and jobs in exchange for safety and a new life.

I met Neineh through Exodus Refugee Immigration, where he works as an Employment Specialist for the many families attempting to merge into the new cultures around them. He's young—not yet thirty years old—and an International Studies graduate from an Indiana university and has all the passion and philosophy of a top campaigner. But then, that's the essence of Neineh—a campaigner.

It doesn't take long to realize his job is more than helping people find jobs in warehouses, hospitality or meat-packing plants, interpreting conversations with employers or doing the administrative work—his whole heart is tied up with these people. When I ask him about Burma, he talks of the sixty-three-year-long civil war, the fear of government persecution, and the struggle to live an everyday life, which is what drives him to share that responsibility with the refugees he meets. He talks sensitively about healing their pain and doing all he can to see their dreams of freedom, happiness, and development become a reality.

A good number of refugee families in Indianapolis live in affordable apartment complexes close to others from their home countries. Their children probably go to the same schools and they meet each other at the nearby grocery store. In many ways this gives families a chance to feel safe and the same. Their accents aren't different here, what they cook isn't exotic; they share some common ground. And yet on the other side of this, the refugees are here, but they're not here, they're in America but they're not part of mainstream communities. That small line of separation starts to form. The refugees live over there; we live over here—our paths rarely, if ever, cross.

Making friends is an art; making friends across language and cultural barriers demands another kind of resolve that comes from sheer patience and the allowance of information found in websites like the UN's refugee agency to cut through our preset ideas and see what's true and what's familiar. One thing I've learned from Esther, all the women's collectives, and Neineh is that those in need aren't necessarily work shy. If anything they simply want an opportunity to work and contribute something of themselves to society too.

* * *

Fair trade is the humane and ethical approach to trading that became popular when Fairtrade the organization started to grow in momentum as its blue and green certification trademark logo became more and more prominent in stores beginning in 2002. The idea to help farmers, especially small farmers, and workers improve their quality of life by buying their goods at fair prices is not only simple, but may help undo the damage of global trade laws.

It seems strange to think that my choice of bananas or chocolate can have such far-reaching effects. And yet despite the numbing complexities of trade laws and regulations, consumers still hold a lot of sway. Fair trade fruit and treats may be more expensive than the store's own brand, but the cost difference brings with it development and empowerment in the producer's home country. The Fairtrade Foundation works to fight poverty and injustice through trade and consequently see improvements in and the lives and income of farmers and workers.[3]

Catholic Agency for Overseas Development (CAFOD), Christian Aid, Oxfam, Traidcraft, World Development Movement, and National Federation of Women's Institutes began the Fairtrade Foundation in 1992. They wanted to see a world in which there can be justice and sustainable development in trade. They sought out partnerships that gave ordinary civilians some say and a chance to earn a decent living. It's an idea that has continued to grow, with nine new members and even a new ethical clothing campaign.

Fair trading of clothing isn't a new deal. Most of us remember when a well-known U.S. clothes store had to wrangle itself out of a PR nightmare when it was exposed that their clothes came from factories run like sweatshops. There was an outcry. People complained and picketed. They stopped shopping at the store and told their friends not to either. The company's stocks went down and so did its sales.

But, why *then*? People wore clothes made in those same conditions all the time, so what was different then? People. And their stories. When we don't know where our clothes come from, they're just objects, just something to be used until we're bored. When a newspaper runs a story about the origins of our t-shirts and the people who make them, clothing stops being about objects.

People aren't things. Even when we don't know them or don't particularly like them, they're still more than things. When people are made to sit at sewing machines and swelter with few breaks, no fresh air or windows, and barely any water, and they aren't paid a fair wage, we know something is dislocated. Robots and flashy slimline computers can be switched on with hardly any human contact to produce masses of whatever it is we request. People, on the other hand, have souls. They have pain thresholds. They have human dignity.

And so our t-shirts and where they came from take us to young women who have left their rural homes, barely able to string a sentence of English together, but with poverty so dire waiting for them that they will sit for sixteen hours, seven days a week and will wreck their bodies for the few dollars that this work will give them. Because we like t-shirts, dresses, off the shoulder shirts, pinstripe pants, and several versions of the same style of cardigan, and we like them cheap, manufacturers will oblige us and cut corners and people's livelihoods.

We'll become enraged by this cruelty and talk about how angry we are when we're having socially conscious and driven conversations over dinner with friends, but on Saturday we'll go to the mall and get that bargain of a dress for going out, because even though we care, just one dress can't hurt, right?

* * *

Cotton is a precious product. Maybe we don't think of it as precious, but we love our favorite jeans, t-shirts, bed sheets, pillows, and towels. It's grown all over the world, and in West Africa particularly. Around ten million West African farmers grow this "white gold," which some say should be their ticket out of years of poverty, but instead it has produced very few riches. This isn't because there's anything wrong with the cotton, but rather it indicates what is wrong with trade laws that promised these farmers a chance to be a player in the world market.

Trade can be highbrow and complex, but justice is simple. When developed countries heavily subsidize their cotton farmers ($32 billion over the last nine years) and export their cotton to Benin, Burkina Faso, Chad and Mali in West Africa, they can lower their cotton prices, which means locals will buy their products rather than the more expensive homegrown ones[4]—leaving West Africa's cotton farmers with a suffocated economy. But this isn't just in cotton. It is in shoes, sugar, and steel.[5] Somehow trade went from being a shared experience of countries giving and taking to a few deciding the livelihood of the world's 2.8 billion who are living in poverty.

When the earthquake hit Haiti at the beginning of 2010, we were all stunned. Earthquake damage isn't new, but we were stunned by Haiti. The country's poverty and weak infrastructure came glaring at us from our TVs as news reporters stood beside thousands of broken people and the 250,000 to 300,000 dead, who had been living in hardship for ages—it's just we hadn't noticed much before. The world's response was swift. We gave donations, wrote pop songs to raise money, held concerts, made documentaries, sent medical teams, tried to adopt groups of children lost in the chaos…and tried to keep selling our rice.

Haitians grow their own rice; they have had rice fields in the fertile Artibonite Valley for generations, but somehow there was more United States Agency for International Development (USAID), tax-subsidized rice on the Haitian market than anything grown locally.[6] Farmers like Jonas Deronzil watched as their goods sat in warehouses unable to compete with the cheap and cheerful foreign imports.

Haiti is still quite rural and the poorest country in the Western hemisphere. Between 66 percent and 80 percent of the citizens are small farmers, or peasants as they call themselves. And yet despite having this farming skill, Haiti imports 50 percent of what they eat. Of the nine million people in Haiti, 2.4 million are in a grave food crisis and 9 percent of children under five suffer malnutrition.[7]

In 1986 and 1995 Haiti took out loans with International Monetary Fund (IMF), the international group that writes trade laws and decides its own terms, in exchange that they would lower import tariffs to as low as 3 percent. The result was lost farmer livelihoods, new employment in sweatshops, mass migration to the capital Port-au-Prince, and movement into sloping slums built on dangerous land. When the earthquake came, it didn't take much to level homes.

The eighth target for the UN's Millennium Development Goals is global partnership development. It's also the one goal that is struggling to make progress, with talks and conferences ending with indecision and calendar updates for more talks.

We inherited trade from the ancient world; it's how the world has always worked—from the grass roots of neighborhood markets to the stock exchange market floors in New York and London. Markets can be unruly places—just try going window-shopping in a Moroccan souk and you'll soon see the necessity for order. And so we made trade laws. The trade laws that are in place demand that poor countries open their markets to the world and sell their public services like electricity. The laws forbid them from subsidizing their own farmers (while the developed countries are allowed and enthusiastically encouraged to) and put high tariffs on these countries so they can only afford to export raw materials, like cotton.

Fair trade and free trade are not the same things despite what images they conjure. The trade laws promote free trade, which means trading without interference from any governments. If you disagree with the laws set, the dispute process is long and difficult because you're seen to be obstructing trade. If you still disagree you'll be penalized in the most severe form—trade sanctions. And to lose your ability to trade is to kill your country slowly and certainly.

Trade laws are written and enforced by those with power—World Trade Organization (WTO), World Bank (WB), and International Monetary Fund (IMF). In other words, 99 percent of developed countries make and write the trade laws, with our Western interests at heart. When we realize that these major groups and bodies are supposed to be the defenders of order and equity, we see how far we've fallen short of the mark. For what hope do a country and its people really have when their interests have already been sacrificed for the good of the 99 percent?

There's an old saying, "give a man a fish; you have fed him for today. Teach a man to fish, and you have fed him for a lifetime." It's a hopeful saying and is a favorite of lots of charities, probably because it offers a dignity in having a skill that brings food and finances to your family and the pride that you have a skill someone else will trade you for. Kiva is an organization that hopes to give people that opportunity. Kiva is a micro-financer, giving loans to individuals who are so poor, banks in their own country won't give them credit. These individuals then use the money to start their small businesses and pay the loans back.

It was Muhammad Yunus's idea in Bangaladesh in the late 1970s, and it was copied all over the world. His Grameen Bank has helped eight million of Bangladesh's poorest people.[8] But is putting the poorest of poor in more debt for credit what we should be doing? Are we making sure they understand investment and interest? Will they be ready when the loans must be repaid?

Microfinancing has its critics and questions; it has its limits, but it also says clearer than any wishful thinking that people want to see something done. Kiva is based in San Francisco but still bridges countries and communities. It works by individuals like you and me finding possible hopefuls to invest in. The average investment is $70. With a $175 loan, twenty-seven-year-old Pendo Luisi was able to open a café in Dar-es-Salaam.[9] People can lend money in teams to offer bigger loans to others, keeping in contact online about their progress and development.

This isn't to say everyone is so noble. More and more newspapers have reported new unregulated microlenders who are exploiting the poor and pushing them into even deeper debt. Poverty traps 2.8 billion people around the world—2.8 billion people earn less than $2 a day. And yet we are still finding ways to take what they don't have. Something is painfully wrong.

In the Old Testament, God gives Israel a custom on Mount Sinai. He tells them that the forty-ninth year in Canaan will be their year of jubilee. It will be the year when debts are cancelled, pawned property can be returned, and slaves can get their freedom (see Leviticus 25). It was a revolutionary concept because it reminded Israel that life was bigger than ownership. It reminded them that generosity and fairness were more of what God was interested in.

The word jubilee comes from the Hebrew word *yobel*, which means "ram." A ram's horn was the one used as a trumpet that would be blown loudly throughout the towns and cities to announce the beginning of the jubilee. A ram was also the animal of sacrifice. It was the animal that God gave to Abraham to take Isaac's place on the mountain in Moriah, and it's what the Israelites gave as their prize offering on the Day of Atonement.

There's sacrifice in freeing someone from his or her debts. There's sacrifice in giving up that property to the homeless. There's sacrifice in tracing the origin of your clothes and checking to be sure eight-year-olds didn't make them. The developing world is in debt. It is in such chronic debt that 128 of the poorest countries owe the developed world $3.7 trillion. Another forty-eight poor countries owe $168 billion.[10] The developing world owes us a phenomenal amount of money. Money that could be used in more lasting ways like development and restoration, in education and medicine, in homes and trade—in general well-being. But that would need debts to be cancelled. It would need forgiveness of failure, a jubilee of sorts.

I know of some coffee shop owners who are passionate about good coffee and who have real doubts about Fairtrade (the certification body, not fair trade the humane practice). Their questions hinge on the quality of the products that are farmed without variation every year and the inflated prices that are paid to these farmers. Fairtrade protects the producers from exploitation and environmental awareness in their farming method, but they do not necessarily ensure quality, especially as many of the products are mass-produced.[11] And these coffee shop owners aren't alone. Some believe that Fairtrade is merely a way of reducing consumer guilt and is a clever marketing concept.[12]

I wonder at the truth in that—that we are all riddled with guilt. We read these facts and statistics and compare our lives; we try to fit a global perspective into our minds and are overwhelmed by it. And when we're overwhelmed we feel powerless to all the injustices that come in so many different shapes. And then we feel guilty, and we withdraw.

But this isn't about guilt; this is about compassion. This is about seeing another's life and empathizing and sharing what we have and not loathing our own lives or the material security we've been born into. It's about doing the best we can in severe circumstances.

A system promising customers that these are "fairer goods" may be imperfect, but it's love in action. It's turning the brutally exclusive club of world trade upside down and giving people that small chance. In the middle of all of these debates are individuals who simply want to eat, drink clean water, live in a house, see their children grow and be educated, remain safe from disease, love, and marry. Like us, they are individuals who just want to live their lives.

Jesus and the poor crop up a lot throughout the gospels. Jesus and his thoughts on fair trade are more scant. That isn't to say they're impossible to find. Perhaps one of his most celebrated verses is: "Blessed are those who hunger and thirst for righteousness, for they will be filled" (Matthew 5:6). We're not just being told a reality here but invited to be different. To be the kind of people who are so determined to see justice and fairness given out freely, it turns us inside out, the way only true hunger or thirst can.

These are not just supposed to be poetic images but a grainy illustration of the human body at its most desperate point. We know what it feels like to feel thirsty, to go for a run or do yard work outside on a summer day and be panting for a drink. But the word "thirst" in the Greek is *dipsao*, which literally means a strong thirst, like what we would have if we were dehydrated. Dehydration is a devastating experience. "Your throat dries out and seems to close up on itself, your lips and tongue grow thick, crack and blacken."¹³ So Jesus compares the desperation for justice with one of the most painful human experiences. If we are to see justice, then it needs to go deeper than just making us feel slightly uncomfortable.

Jesus wasn't a trade union representative, but when he sent out the other seventy-two men, he gave them different points of advice. One stuck with me the most: ". . . the worker deserves his wages" (Luke 10:7). He never went into detail about how those wages should be given, when or how much exactly, but it's clear Jesus thought it fair and just to pay someone for the work they've done. That's not to say we aren't supposed to carefully consider ideas and policies, especially when dealing with money, economics, and livelihoods, but when it comes to basic human need, Jesus' response was always verb-centered. It was nearly always about taking action: "You give them something to eat" (Luke 9:13) or "my child, get up" (Luke 8:54)!

There is an example in which Jesus was faced directly with the question of work and ethics. When he meets Zaccheus in Jericho, the chief tax collector is up in a sycamore fig tree trying to get a better look at the famous rabbi. Jesus arranges to have dinner with him, but Zaccheus immediately confesses his corruption and instantly gives back what he has stolen. He doesn't wait for Jesus to mention that he knows he has exploited his position and those with the least. He confesses and he makes amends.

Maybe being in God's company does that; maybe it makes us more aware of the sufferings of others and our actions or inaction that has put them there. When Jesus was faced with a large crowd of hungry people, he took the five loaves of bread and two fish, looked up to heaven, gave thanks, and broke them. He gave them to the disciples to hand out to everyone. It started with five loaves and two fish and fed five thousand souls. It was a miracle, not only for the otherworldly math shown here, but that Jesus got people to share. Seeing the example of someone giving up their dinner inspired them. They shared until there were twelve baskets of leftovers (see Luke 9:10-17). He was asking them as he asks us, "What do you have? Let's use what you have."

It's the same today. Justice is about giving developing countries the room to use what they have to create provision and meet their needs. Maybe it's in this kind of relationship that we can see where trade and the international community can actually work—where people are given a chance to build up, be imaginative, strengthen their community's economy, and enjoy mutual respect of having repaid the assistance.

Perhaps grassroots justice starts when we buy those coffee beans, or paper bracelets, or tell our friends a little bit about who these individuals are, or buy from our local farmers too. We start to stir things from the roots right up to where the needs are. Sometimes we crave huge bombastic things to happen like wealthy countries to become more selfless instead of mainly protecting the interests of the rich (and rightly so), and recognize we live in a global community where our rules and regulations affect others. Yet, sometimes lasting change comes when we all make that little decision of who we buy our coffee from and where we get this year's Christmas presents.

Recycle, reuse, reduce

You've heard it a million times, but I'm not talking about those plastic bins you leave outside your house once a week (although those are a good thing as well).

Follow in the footsteps of the women in Uganda and reuse those sheets of paper that your printer has accidentally spit out with some eight-digit alpha numeric code comprehensible only to those of its own "printer" kind.

Or reuse the copy paper at work that has printed out landscape when it was supposed to be portrait or vice versa. All this paper that would have ended up in a landfill somewhere can make great to-do lists, notepads, and scratch paper!

Keep trade fair

If you can't buy local, buy Fairtrade.

Fairtrade insures farmers in foreign countries receive a fair wage for their work.

Call your local grocery story and request fair trade foods. You can actually taste the fair wages in them!

Go to:
http://www.transfairusa.org

Buy a goat

Oh, I see you live in an apartment. Well I didn't mean buy a goat for yourself (but if you decide to, I know people who have grown up with them, and I cannot discourage any pet ownership more).

Oxfam sells goats and other animals and services that you can purchase for a family in a developing country. These make great gifts for a friend or for a soon-to-become friend from a remote district in Nepal.

Find out more at:
http://www.oxfamamericaunwrapped.com

Support the women in Uganda: Mama Pamba

Anyone's birthday coming up? Why not make the jewelry present a little different this year?

Take a look at some of the work Meaningful Volunteer is doing with their wonderful collectives like Mama Pamba and The Meaningful Shop. Take your pick of handmade earrings, necklaces, and bracelets made by women in Uganda.

Sometimes it's nice to know who made what you're or the birthday person's wearing, and quite often it's just as inexpensive as your most recent clearance shelf purchase.

Take a look at: http://www.meaningfulvolunteer.org

Oyster world

The world is a big place, and it starts where we are.

Traveling, even if it's just outside your state (or even your *neighborhood*), could be a complete eye opener. You might just meet people you love or clash with. They might disagree with your views about this world and how to deal with it.

Keep your peace. Buy them a cup of coffee and have a chat. Don't try to convince them of anything; simply get to know them a bit more.

Keep the dialogue flowing.

Shop locally

There are people in your hometown who are making the most amazing gifts and growing some of the tastiest foods. Why not give them a bit of your hard-earned cash? A little in their pocket saves a lot in transportation costs for foods and goods that have to fly in from other countries.

Check out your local farmer's market. Cheese, fruit, and vegetables have never tasted so good.

3
DIAMONDS *are* FOREVER

"May God bless you with holy anger at injustice, oppression, and exploitation of people, so that you may tirelessly work for justice, freedom, and peace among all people."

—ST. FRANCIS OF ASSISI[1]

Marilyn Monroe, Audrey Hepburn, and Shirley Bassey all have one thing in common. Not their illustrious lives and sometimes height-defying hair or makeup, but their depicted love of a certain glittering gem.

The diamond has been a symbol of love and the promise of a sweet wedding to come since De Beers fashioned a marketing campaign with the very savvy American advertising company N. W. Ayers and Son in 1939. Their plan was to encourage hundreds of men to spend three months of their salaries on jeweled engagement rings—and it worked.[2] With a good mixture of Hollywood starlets wearing the gems, contemporary art exhibiting added sparkles, and lectures being given to convince young women that no courtship was complete without that sparkly ring, De Beers and Ayers and Son managed to cement the diamond as the ultimate love offering.[3]

And yet the history of the diamond goes back to ancient India where it was first recorded 3,000 years ago for its ability to retract light. After that it was used either for decoration or more importantly as a talisman against evil or to be worn when going into battle.[4]

The ancient Greeks believed diamonds were tears of the gods and splinters from falling stars.[5] They were also the ones that gave the jewel its name *adámas*, which means "unbreakable," "unalterable," and "untameable." Its renowned hardness became interpreted as a superior strength—even magic. Plato even wrote about diamonds as beings with celestial spirits inside them.[6]

By the Dark Ages myths and folklore about diamonds started to spring up all over old Europe. St. Hildegarde tended to hold a diamond in one hand while making the sign of the cross to heal wounds and sicknesses.[7] Later on, some people even got into the habit of swallowing diamonds to be cured. In 1532, Pope Clement VII was prescribed fourteen spoonfuls of crushed gems (diamonds too), which was probably the cause of his unhappy demise.[8]

Things started changing in the Middle Ages, when European mine owners realized the potential of their treasures. Royalty began wearing diamonds to highlight their courage and invincibility. And in 1477, Archduke Maximilian of Austria proposed to Mary of Burgundy with the first documented diamond engagement ring. Mine owners soon spun the myth that diamonds were poisonous and so reduced the chances of their wishful workers swallowing them and smuggling them out of the mines.[9]

But it wasn't until diamonds were discovered south of the Orange River in South Africa that the diamond fever that we now know took hold.[10] In 1867, a Boer farmer named Daniel Jacobs passed on a "glittering pebble" to a neighbor and began the South African diamond rush.[11] The fever that followed was a high one that further split open the gap between those with and those without faster than any other mineral.

The 2006 movie *Blood Diamond* probably best captures the human cost of these stones. The story follows an African fisherman, Mende, his European diamond smuggler accomplice, Danny, and an American journalist, Maddy, in their trails across Sierra Leone on the eve of civil war. In 143 minutes we are given a glimpse into the mayhem and conflict diamonds have financed.

In 1991 a war began in Sierra Leone between the rebel group Revolutionary United Front (RUF) and the current government. The RUF kidnapped children and forced them into their army to fight in a war that would last eleven years. The bewildering thing is that the RUF then spent most of the civil war brutally victimizing the ordinary working men, women, and children. Local, illiterate villagers often had their hands or arms amputated with a machete to hinder them from voting against the RUF, and also so that they could no longer work their subsistence farms. Without the hands to work, they were essentially being sentenced to a prolonged death. Adults and children were forced to work in diamond mines in Kono to find the very stones that would be sold and sent into Europe in exchange for arms.

The movie doesn't shy away from the dark reality of the war. Drugs were used to keep the children desensitized and robotic in their killings. They were given cocaine, heroin, and speed to give them courage when entering the fray. It's been said that part of being fully initiated into the rebel group was to eat the still-beating human heart of their victim.

Around 5,000 children were forced to fight, 75,000 civilians were killed, and between 50,000 and 200,000 others died in the conflict, while two million people were displaced.[12] I read these statistics and I wonder where God's voice is in all this madness. I think of the people who have been killed, severely wounded, and made homeless and orphaned. I think of the chaos that reigned and the absolute fear that must have been in every single one of them, and I wonder, where was God's mercy and goodness and justice?

I find it tucked throughout the whole Bible. God is the champion of the poor, the widow, and the orphan. His entire heart is interwoven with people's suffering. Through the prophets and psalms, God tells us the same thing repeatedly: he detests oppression. The writer of Proverbs spells it out clearly when he says, "He who oppresses the poor to increase his wealth and he who gives gifts to the rich—both come to poverty" (22:16). Throughout the Bible, God is the defender of the poor and weak; he's their protector. When we see the riches that were fought over in Sierra Leone, this line fits—even though it was compiled so many centuries before.

It's strange that while Sierra Leone was in chaos, the rest of the world remained fairly quiet. Perhaps it was because of the Bosnian war or the Kosovo conflict that were happening around the same time. Either way Sierra Leonean children were left to kill their families and friends in amphetamine-induced rages.

There are hundreds of wars happening all the time. Some seem louder than others because they get more coverage, but how do we choose what to cover? And what do our choices say about the lives we're interested in looking at? The international stage can be slightly suspect at best, especially when we realize that the West wasn't completely ignorant of what was happening in Sierra Leone. Massive numbers of diamonds were bought and traded between the RUF and the West by being smuggled through Liberia. Liberia made a fortune in diamond sales, despite not having many diamond minerals of its own.[13]

Documentaries about Sierra Leone's brutal and atrocious civil war are all over the Internet, and so are people's comments on it. I stumbled upon one comment that I think captures very well the tension between the West and everywhere else. The person who had written it was furious that the U.S. or the UN was being asked to help sort out a mess that Africans had created. Another asked why after fifty years of independence and trillions of dollars in aid, Africa has been unable to live peacefully?[14] As simplistic as this person was being, I was left wondering how many of us haven't asked the same questions. How much should we be involved in battles happening in different time zones to people we don't and never will know—and in battles we did not personally cause?

One thing I really like about *Blood Diamond* is that it asks brutally honest questions and forces statements and opinions to the surface. When the trio are trying to escape from danger, they argue about going back into the battle to find Mende's son. Maddy asks why, when the whole country is at war, should they return for one person? We echo this sentiment in the real world, where war is nearly always seen in collectives. The number of casualties comes in groups. The number of deaths appears in groups. The number and types of weapons are listed in large sums. And this is true: in war there are massive losses, so we count them together. But in those numbers, there are individual people. Each of those is one, with a name, a history. When we look at lump sums it's easier to disconnect because the figures are insurmountable and they stop being human and start being numbers, tallies on a sheet.

I think social justice is a bit like this. We deal with such huge, sweeping figures it overwhelms and depresses. But the whole crowd is still made up of individuals. Individuals are what we can relate to and sometimes all we can manage. When Jesus spoke about leaving the flock of ninety-nine to save the one lost sheep, he probably wasn't relating it to war and its numbers.

But perhaps the same principles can be applied. People are people; their lives are valuable—each and every one.

Maybe we are supposed to be involved in other people's battles and stand with those who are being battered and remind them that we haven't forgotten them or cast them off to a graph or table of figures. Maybe by remembering they are individuals, we won't be numb to the suffering that is very real for many people.

"Will God ever forgive us for what we've done to each other?" This is the question Danny asks the man in the film who loves and adopts broken former child soldiers. And I see it is a question about the smuggling and trading of conflict diamonds. It is a question about governments and rebel groups that oppress and punish innocent people who have no means of fighting back. It is a question to countries that sell arms, knowing they are going to destroy and maim. And it is a question to those of us who choose not to think about such unpleasant things.

Jesus answers the question in the absolution he offers us on the cross, and that brings a measure of peace and hope, but we still have our part to play in absolving each other of our debts (see Matthew 6:12-14). Jesus knew the full extent of the sins and the horrors to come and he already had the answer and the way out—a clean page. Forgiveness. Perhaps it seems too uncomplicated to say forgiveness will sort out these crimes against humanity that are still seeing Charles Taylor, Liberia's former President and the RUF's leader, on trial in The Hague.[15] Yet, perhaps we have made forgiveness seem too easy. Forgiveness demands responsibility of action and involvement in something wrong; it demands the humility to see that uncomfortable and necessary change takes place.

In 2003, the Kimberley Process Certification Scheme was introduced by the UN General Assembly to try to trace the origins of rough diamonds and limit the number of blood diamonds being mixed in with legitimate diamonds that once bought on the market and polished become exactly the same.[16] Yet, eight years later, after seventy-five countries have renewed their commitment to KPCS, it hasn't totally fixed the problems. The growing questions over Zimbabwe's diamonds and the dubious ease with which anyone can "buy" a KPCS stamp leave little confidence that this method alone can provide the lasting change that's needed.[17]

Zimbabwe's government and military have been all over the media for their crimes. Zimbabwe has breached hundreds of human rights, but none so blatantly as the killings in the diamond reserves of Marange, which is on the border with Mozambique. The Marange diamond fields have the single most concentrated area of diamonds anywhere in the world. In 2006, the government took over the fields and hundreds of civilian miners were killed by attacking dogs or were machine-gunned from helicopters. After just one attack, over 200 bodies were brought to the Mutare morgue.[18]

Human Rights Watch has recorded that mass killings, torture, beatings, and forced labor are the order of life in Zimbabwe today.[19] And yet despite this, $150 million worth of diamonds have still managed to be smuggled out of the country since 2003. The fact that the KPCS is still certifying Zimbabwe's diamonds as "conflict free" cries of injustice.[20] We know people are dying. We know that most of the money that comes from diamonds goes to only a few at the top. It doesn't always trickle down and buy antiretroviral medicine for those succumbing to AIDS. It doesn't always build schools and give children a hope out of poverty. It doesn't always care for housing or reach the poor in any way, and yet we turn away. We give it space in newspapers and we debate about it on TV; we condemn the leaders in highbrow intellectual conversations, but KPCS has still been slow to revoke their certificate from Zimbabwe—because Zimbabwe has diamonds in one of the best diamond mines ever.

But it's not only war and outright bloodshed that should get our attention. The Kimberley Process was written to restore our trust in the entire diamond industry, but it's still fairly quiet on labor-related issues, environmental concerns, and the violence used by "recognized" governments. While researching this topic, I found a video that plays as an ode to Sierra Leone and asks some real questions about the limits to the KPC industry trademark. In the video a group of small African children hold pitch hammers to dig along the narrow, dark walls of a mine. It looks like a scene out of a workhouse in a Dickensian story except these children wear barely any clothes and have the most dilated pupils I've ever seen from the lack of sunlight. It's disturbing because they look right at you and it's disturbing because they don't look human—they look alien.

At dawn in Sierra Leone, children and adults will head to the mines, which look more like mud pools, and spend the rest of the burning day up to their waists in water, hunched over their round sieve pans, scouring for diamonds. This form of mining is called alluvial mining, as the diamonds have come up to the surface. First the dirt is dug back, and then water rises from underneath to make these small pools; then the sieving can begin.

This is an inefficient method, but it is a cheap method because labor is cheap. A lot of these mines are located near internally displaced people's camps (IDPs), so the owners have easy access to manual laborers. Their workers live in the camps with barely any options and few ways out. They live in cramped, squalid conditions with disease, little to no sanitation, and abounding hunger. For the workers who live hand to mouth, their biggest needs are food and water—and that's what they're given. The mine owners rarely pay them in money.[21] The workers are given food and lodging; if they find a diamond, they may get a small bonus.

Unlike during the civil war, the overseers do not bear guns in obvious display, but as there isn't any work for miles around, the workers will not risk their jobs by attempting to steal anyway. Usually the workers pan for diamonds naked to prevent them being tempted to try to sneak a diamond out. Global Witness estimates there are about one million diamond diggers who earn less than $1 a day.[22]

International Rescue Mission (IRM) has a short two-minute video on the mines. They end it by mentioning that the children were hidden from view when the overseer saw them and their cameras. He knew that Americans wouldn't want to see the children working. He knew it would make these foreign aid workers and any of their viewers uncomfortable to watch children laboring. And we're left to wonder if that's the reputation that precedes us—a people who will turn away. A people who will change the channel or who will stop the video—because we have that unbelievable freedom to involve ourselves in something or to pull back and switch off.

But I wonder how long we can continue to do that and whether increased access to information has changed our ability to hide from and ignore news like this. We have so many portholes to foreign countries on TV, the radio, and the Internet. We know the names of their cities and governments, we know if they're at peace or war, and we know about the conditions they live in. But, I don't think we've become a news-obsessed species because we're nosy—rather, we are interested in our world and those in it. We do want to know what happens in mud pool mines in West Africa. Even if knowing breaks us in the process.

Isaiah said a lot of profound things, but one stands out brightly: "The people walking in great darkness have seen a great light; on those living in the land of the shadow of death a light has dawned" (Isaiah 9:2). There is still hope. Regardless of how deep the darkness has become, there really are those who can't stomach the intricate injustices in the diamond industry and they've not only wept over it; they've been moved and acted on it.

When I first read about "conflict-free" diamonds, I thought the whole concept was a bit contradictory. Wasn't Africa just coming up for air after long years of bloody wars in Angola, the Ivory Coast, Liberia, and Sierra Leone over those diamonds? How could any of them be conflict free? But then again, maybe these wars have been the catalyst for so many to try to clean up the industry.

Brilliant Earth sells diamond rings, earrings, and pendants, but the difference is they know the source of their diamonds. They know the names and details of those who mine the diamonds in Namibia; like Fairtrade coffee, they insist that their mineworkers are paid well and work in safe, secure conditions. The workers not only have steady employment in mining, cutting, and polishing the diamonds, but Brilliant Earth has mapped out "the diamond-funded Prevention Care and Support Program," offering education, health care advice, and treatment to combat HIV/AIDS.[23] And that's another thing about companies like Brilliant Earth—they're not solely concerned about the product, but the people who spend hours in the red earth getting it out. Most mine workers just want to work to earn money for food, housing, medical care, and education. For them, the available industry is diamonds, and despite its reputation, they still need the work.

Diamonds aren't just an African marvel anymore. Canada has its own mines and is offering the world environmentally-aware mining, conflict-free diamonds.[24] In February of 2011, a seventy-eight-carat diamond was found at the Ekati mine site near Yellowknife.[25] In layman's terms, this means the stone is as big as the top joint of an adult's thumb. But this wasn't the most interesting fact. BHP Billiton, which mines at both the Ekati and Diavik sites in the Northwestern territories, did something that marks a hopeful shift in mining between owners and workers. They made a point to recruit and retain the people of the north in their workforces for their tracking skills and knowledge of the environment and land around and have provided them with in-house training for further development.[26] Maybe it was only a marketing ploy to get our compassion, but it's a far cry from the forced resettlement of people that we've seen happen scores of times in history the moment minerals have been found.

We all know, thanks to Physics class, that diamonds form through a geological process over millions of years in the dark earth until they come closer to the surface where we can dig for them. Their age and their hardness (they can cut glass) make them so valuable and almost mythical. But what's more of a surprise is that scientists have been busy perfecting the art of growing diamonds in labs. Since scientists first discovered the diamond was essentially pure carbon in 1797, they've been trying to recreate this natural phenomenon and recently have managed to make it work.

From Florida to Calgary, diamonds have been grown either copying the earth's high-pressure high-temperature (HPHT) or the chemical vapor deposition (CVD), where diamonds are grown like seeds in pink cases.[27] It all sounds a bit like science fiction to be able to grow diamonds, but lab diamonds aren't just being made to stem the mining demand for jewelry. They are also being used for scientific and medical developments. A lot of these man-made gems will be used in medicine and computing from future computer chips and lasers to frictionless medical replacement joints.[28]

* * *

My sister Anna and I both love films from the '30s, '40s, and '50s. There's something about the style, fashion, and melodrama that's fun to watch. One of our favorites is probably *Gentlemen Prefer Blondes* because of Marilyn Monroe's amazing ability to scarcely blink throughout the entire film (honestly!). She sings a famous song in it that became something of a mantra for women everywhere: "Diamonds Are a Girl's Best Friend." As Marilyn sings in her hot pink dress it's impossible to miss the huge diamond necklace and bracelets glittering around her neck and wrists as she calls out "Tiffany" and "Cartier." The song, as well as the jewelers mentioned, will always be firmly embedded in our minds.

With songs like this and Shirley Bassey's, "Diamonds Are Forever," which still popularize diamonds, it's hard to imagine an alternative for an engagement ring—but that is exactly what is starting to happen all over the U.S. and parts of Europe.

When my old roommate Christina got engaged, her fiancé didn't give her the traditional solitaire ring but a band he designed made from Oklahoma's Eastern redbud wood with a pearl set between two silver leaves. He had a message for her engraved inside and gave it to her while they were eating baklava in our backyard in Nashville.

When my husband and I got engaged he proposed to me with an antique white gold ring with a small Mississippi pearl in the place where a diamond used to be. People's reactions when they see it are always funny. On the one hand they're delighted because it's so different and unique and on the other there's this look of genuine confusion as to what happened to the diamond.

Frank Ladner is a carpenter, but a different sort. In addition to rustic furniture, he makes wooden rings using an old bentwood method with traditional tools and techniques. He uses native storm-blown trees, fallen limbs, scraps or cutoff that would otherwise be wasted to create his rings and sometimes adds turquoise or crushed mother of pearls for gems.[29] When he sends the rings out he packages them in little brown boxes wrapped in twine with tubs of polishing wax to keep the wood bright. They need to be treated carefully, but there's very little that can beat Indian rosewood.

Wooden, pearl, jade, or plain tattoo rings have all steadily become options for brides and grooms. Whether it's for environmental or social issues, there are definitely more alternatives and ways in which we can be involved in our huge world and its even bigger issues than there were before.

Diamonds are irrevocably interwoven with human life. When used fairly they provide employment, trade, income and the essentials: school, hospitals, homes, sanitation, food, and water—

the same needs that exist in both a community in Canada's Northwest or in West Africa. But we cannot look past the fact that those at the bottom of the diamond chain tend to be the most vulnerable—the widows, orphans, and poor. They live hand to mouth, in or under poverty. We're being asked to notice them, to put their needs before our wants and maybe see a shift in the heavyweight industries from oppression to fairness.

Diamonds are probably one of the most beautiful and beastly things in this world. Beastly for how they have compromised our souls with desensitized greed, violence, and brutality, beautiful because there is something strangely alluring about them. I started writing this chapter thinking diamonds were inherently wrong, but I see now they can be a livelihood, a lifeline. Diamonds aren't necessarily the problem. It's what we do and the decisions we make for wealth and power that cause the problem. Maybe now it's our turn to remember the human cost involved and to ask questions about the source of our stones and give voice to those whose own aren't being heard.

Trace your diamond

I know it might take a bit of work, especially with the amount of information floating around on cyberspace, but it's really worth it.

The best way to pour water on the fire is to not purchase any at all. This idea may seem a bit out of the ordinary and might really challenge some of you, but it's truly the best way to combat this huge injustice.

A real gem of an alternative

There are plenty of beautiful alternatives out there. If you're proposing to someone or planning on being proposed to, run a quick Internet search of non-traditional engagement rings and pick something you like. Keep in mind though that while diamonds are the biggest culprits of these conflicts, there are other gems that are also causing problems. Make sure you verify that your stone is not from a conflict region. And ladies, most of these gems are less expensive, so you may not be waiting around for so long for your mister to pop the question if he doesn't have to save for years upon years to buy you the perfect ring!

Start your search here:
http://www.stoutwoodworks.com
http://www.touchwoodrings.com

Become a jewel thief

If your heart is set on a diamond, first, raid your grandmother's jewelry (suggestion: ask her nicely first) and see if there's something your family already owns that can be reset. I have a couple friends who have done just that. It gives you a one of a kind ring, you'll have produced less greenhouse gases by using a stone that's already here, and you'll probably end up with a ring that is worth significantly more than what you had to pay to have it made.

If that doesn't work (i.e. if your cane-wielding grandma catches you snooping and chases you away from her jewelry box), contact an ethical diamond provider such as Brilliant Earth.

http://www.brilliantearth.com

Spread the word

Making people aware is really half the battle here. Now, don't go up to everyone in your workplace who is wearing a diamond on his or her finger and accuse him or her of murder. That's not nice. But do casually make people aware of the war that is waging to bring these stones to our local jewelers. Bring the topic up in conversations. Have talks with any of your friends who might be planning to purchase one. All you can do is plant the idea in their minds. The rest is up to them.

Surf the net

During your fifteen-minute coffee break today or tomorrow, take some time to read through some websites of conflict diamond campaigns.

Global Witness and World Vision are two organizations that are fighting against conflict diamonds. This might be a good place to start. If you're moved by what they're doing, send a few dollars their way.

http://www.globalwitness.org
http://www.worldvision.org

Hang onto your phone

Yes we all know the iPhone 4 is really, really, really nice. Even I admittedly want one. However, if your 3G or 3GS or even 2G is still kicking, it's best to keep it around for a while longer. The materials that are fueling the conflicts aren't only those pretty glittery things we wear on our fingers, ears, and around our necks. There is also an increasing amount of cobalt being sourced from conflict regions. Cobalt is the main ingredient in the long-life batteries that power many of our portable devices.[30]

Just party

Step 1) Buy CDs or MP3's of musicians who are creating socially conscious work. You may have never heard of some of them, but they are making some great tunes. Emmanuel Jal, the Flobots, State Radio, and Sierra Leone's Refugee All Stars all have some really wild stories! And they're using these stories to create music that spreads the news of social justice.

Step 2) Invite some friends over. If you don't have any friends, go out to your street and find the closest handful of people and invite them in.

Step 3) Share some hors d'œuvres, turn up the music, and have a good time! Fill your heads with melodies and lyrics that promote justice. Do this enough and these things will become a part of who you are.

4
GOD BLESS *the* CHILD

Part of seeing poverty doesn't just mean having pity or compassion; it means being affected to the point where we are fixated on how we can be part of making it right.

While researching this topic, I found a photo on the Internet that stays with me even when I close my eyes. It's of a skinny, malnutritioned ten-year-old boy. The picture is black and white, but I can see he has cropped brown hair and downturned brown eyes. His sweater is too big and fits loosely around his scrawny neck. But it's the bottle that peeks out from his collar and is secretly attached to his mouth that continues to hold my stare. The bottle is full of a thick, yellow shoemaking glue that would give a novice a migraine for days. For a "street child" in a major city in Colombia, it's the certified way to suppress the incessant hunger pangs and destitution that is his life.

Ana Lalinde's mother is a fairy godmother. She doesn't have wings or a wand but has brought a well of hope to hundreds of street children in Medellín, Colombia. Patricia has nursed, embraced, counseled, and shouted loudly on behalf of children whose voices would otherwise have been lost to the image of street imps that signify neighborhood decay.

This isn't to say children living and working on the street are miniature saints. To survive, they have had to become real-life "Artful Dodgers." They have had to steal and commit crimes for food and, more terrifyingly, to keep their lives.

In the years Patricia worked with street children she would have met those like Jose. Jose Adolfo Guzman is from Tunja, three hours away from Bogotá, where he lived with his father and five-month-old sister after his mother abandoned them. He ran away after his stepmother's beatings became too brutal to bear.[1] He left for the capital in a sugar cane truck and immediately walked into a gang that demanded money from him. He learned how to cheat, lie, steal, and beg with them. He learned how the thick yellow glue quelled hunger and that stronger drugs, like basuco,[2] meant they could survive in "the Claret," an impoverished and crime-riddled neighborhood. He would sleep next to small animals on newspapers to keep warm.

Social workers tell of large gangs and criminals who use the children for everything from begging to running drugs. The children are given drugs to tie them in further, and both girls and boys may be trafficked and used until HIV and AIDS leave them worn and unusable. Sadly, the police are very quiet when it comes to these children. It's been reported that instead of protecting them, whole neighborhoods have banded together to hire hit men to "clean up the streets" and reduce the threat of these small individuals that move about in "gamines" or gangs.[3]

It's worth mentioning that for many, the term "street children" has become synonymous with thieves, liars, criminals, danger, and the ruin of their local areas. So getting rid of these "disposable ones"[4] has never been seen as a moral issue. And yet despite its negative connotations a lot of children have accepted the name, as they've accepted being in a gang. It's given them identity and belonging.

"Street children" is a huge blanket term we use, but there is more behind it. Some are "street-working" children who find work in washing windshields or selling fruit or merchandise. They get to go home to their families in shantytowns at night. Others are "children in the street." Their families are even poorer, so they beg and rifle through trash, but again get to go to some kind of home to sleep.⁵ Finally, there are the "children of the street." These children live in the street and learn to survive by committing the crimes that have seen them marginalized and despised.

Life for children of the street is more of an existence. Their homes are with their gangs in their part of the city; to cross boundaries would be to spark a turf attack. Their beds are pieces of cardboard or newspaper and maybe some plastic or an old sack for a blanket. When they do sleep there's the threat of someone stealing their shoes or of being shot at. There's nowhere to wash so they suffer scabies, boils, fleas, and body lice. Their health is vulnerable living in the open and close to garbage, so they pick up diseases like bronchitis and pneumonia.

It is estimated there are between 100 million and 150 million street children in the world.⁶ It is actually quite hard to tell what the exact number is because, as a UNICEF report in 2006 put it, "these children are often though physically visible, ignored, shunned and excluded."⁷ Children live, work, hide, and sleep in shop doorways and alleys in cities all over the world for innumerable reasons but perhaps the most prevailing one is poverty. Throughout the world more than a billion children suffer deprivation in one or more areas, namely safe drinking water, adequate nutrition, decent sanitation, health care, shelter, education, and information.⁸ Without these basic needs met, children are subject to exploitation, abuse, fear, discrimination, starvation, and death.

Colombia, like many other developing countries, has endured a prolonged civil war with violence aimed pointlessly at the poorest of the poor in rural areas. From the 1940s the country was divided by *La Violencia* (the violence) as the two leading parties warred for control. Riots all over the country left at least 180,000 dead.[9] By the 1950s guerrilla groups started to emerge and the Revolutionary Armed Forces of Colombia (FARC) formed in 1964 to fight the government. Through the 1970s and 1980s drugs became more of a factor in the fighting, as the guerrilla and paramilitary groups fought over the coca-growing regions in the south. In 1995, 25,000 people were killed.[10]

In order to protect themselves, families moved in droves to the bigger cities. In 2009 it was reported that direct threats from armed illegal armed forces were the greatest cause for internal displacement.[11] The non-governmental observatory on Human Rights and Displacement (CODHES) has supported this figure, projecting that 4.9 million people would be displaced by 2010.[12] With such increased pressure on housing and employment many of these families built shantytowns just to be in the radius of the city's protection from the guerrilla groups. The result—thousands of people living under the poverty line.

In 2009, the movie *Slumdog Millionaire* topped box office sales and walked away with eight Oscars, including best picture and best director. The story followed one boy's account of outwitting a famous game show by using his life experiences in the slums of Mumbai (Bombay). Somehow the director was able to capture both the tragedy and relentless childlike hope of the boy hero trying to find his childhood friend and love, Latika, who was captured by sex traffickers.

The film has been criticized for being too coincidental, with lots of luck thrown in, but the movie still did what so many organizations campaign and plan, pray and wish for—it brought the story of these children into our lives and straight into all of our faces.

* * *

Ericka Smiley loves life, traveling, and people; she especially loves children. But not just to coo over them or teach them in an inner-city school—she has a dream to build a house of refuge for hurting and neglected children. In 2009 she did her Youth with a Mission (YWAM) Discipleship Training School (DTS) in Bogotá and got to see model houses for kids and how they were organized.

Children at Risk is a house run by YWAM for street children. There are several members of staff in different roles such as counselors, cooks, social workers, community partners, and volunteer builders all helping the house function. The simple practice of morning routines or sitting down for meals is something the children have to become familiar with. For children who have been sniffing glue to suppress hunger or eating only when scraps can be found or a volunteer hands out soup, new habits take a while to form.

But Children at Risk and places like it aren't just projects and ideas; they are homes. They are places children can rest without listening for night watchmen or bullets. There's an order and stability in these places that creates safety that allows them to be children, where they can dream, play, and trust all over again—or perhaps for the very first time.

* * *

I went to the circus once. I can't remember how old I was or where it was, but I do remember I was thrilled. I remember being in the big top, with its peppermint candy stripes and the strong smell of damp hay. I remember sitting on wooden benches and dad buying popcorn and drinks, although I can't remember where my siblings were sitting because we were at the circus and I wanted to take everything in. I wanted to store up the colors, sounds, people's chatter, and the lights.

Maybe it's the influence of Disney's *Dumbo* or just the fact that when you're at the circus anything can happen. Gymnasts twist into funny shapes in sparkly sequined outfits, acrobats leap from stringy wires in the air, elephants march out and make the floor shake, and the ringmaster's voice booms out everywhere. Circuses are magic for most children, even though they are a dying spectacle.

A circus group in Colombia called Circo Para Todos (Circus for All) was founded in 1997 by an English woman named Felicity Simpson. But this circus isn't like the one I went to or the ones that sometimes pass through towns in the U.S.; in this one all the star performers are former street children. Felicity was a circus performer herself. She started with the unicycle then ran off to join a Parisian circus when she was seventeen. She traveled a lot and stopped in Cali, a city in western Colombia and did a duo act with her friend Hector using the unicycle and stilts.

That was when she first met the children and began offering free workshops. None of these children had ever trained before, but their ability convinced her to set up a school. They still hold workshops throughout the different slums like Agua Blanca, Cali's biggest shantytown. Circolombia was their first production and was made up of a bunch of seventeen- to twenty-three-year olds who had learned how to do double somersaults, arabesques in a metal hoop that balances on someone's forehead, and leaps launched off seesaws.

The transformation is inspiring. The children start out as glue-sniffing, itchy-skinned lost souls and graduate as performers and artists. The circus gives them a chance to have a different identity and a different life. Felicity makes a true point when she says, "When they are performing, the public judge them on their new life, not their social past."[13]

When we look at street children and their situation we see pawns, playthings to bigger powers. We don't see that to box them in or doom them as tragic figures, but we understand that what these children have gone, go, and will go through is something no child should ever meet. But maybe Circo Para Todos is a lesson to us in what hope looks like when we start acting on it. Last year the school had eighty-three graduates, many of whom have gone on to the world's best circuses like the Ringling Brothers and Barnum and Bailey, and fifteen of whom have even bought their own houses.[14]

Circo Para Todos promotes the show on the performers' raw talents; they rarely mention the poverty that birthed them. In this way, they tell the children and teenagers they are more than a statistic. But there are other children whose faces we can't let our eyes ignore. There are so many others who haven't been saved by the circus or others and the street is still their story. It's still their present and their future unless someone gets involved.

* * *

My husband and I have some friends named Brad and Rachel Goode. They have three beautiful little daughters. Two are blonde and blue-eyed and one is dark-haired, brown-eyed, and Ugandan. At the time of writing they have just received the judge's permission to adopt little Amelia Mercy Goode and are working on her passport and visa to come home to the States.

We have some other friends, Dominic and Jodi De Souza, who adopted their little boy, TJ, when he was four years old and they were twenty-two and twenty-one years old. People said they were too young to adopt and that at four years old it would be too difficult for TJ to see them as his parents. Five years later he's growing fast into a confident and creative boy who's able to realize his dreams of becoming an actor, seeing as Jodi directs both films and plays and just worked on a project with him called *Kai*.[15]

Most of us don't think of adoption when we consider social justice. Adoption sits in a different realm of family life and is something some people do. Yet there are around thirteen million orphans (who have lost both parents) around the world,[16] and at least 114,562 children are in foster care in need of families in the States.[17] Every day five children die from abuse or neglect, but we don't really hear about it.[18] Every now and again a horror story of child abuse and neglect will appear in the news, like the Kluth couple in Yukon, Oklahoma, who whipped, burned, strangled, and fed pet food to their three adopted children.[19] We hear these stories and we're furious with the parents. We think about those other children waiting in foster care, but after the news has died down, we tend to forget.

Around 70,000 children live in foster care for more than five years. A child will move between two and five foster homes in less than two and a half years. The average age for a child to enter the system is eight years old, despite common belief. Fifty-eight percent of the children in foster homes are children of color. Children can spend at least forty-four months waiting for adoption while more than 80 percent do not have any prospective families willing to adopt. In 2006, 25,000 children aged out of foster care (turned eighteen) and were left to make their way. Most of these young adults become homeless, suffer poor health and unemployment, and will eventually find themselves incarcerated.[20]

None of this is to say we don't adopt. Around 57,466 children were adopted with public agency involvement in 2010, and these adoptions were both domestic and international.[21] Of the children adopted in the U.S. 37 percent came through the foster care system, 38 percent through private agencies, while 27 percent were international adoptions.[22] However maybe there's still something at odds in the way we think about adoption. The children that are hardest to place are still those who are older, have siblings with whom they want to be placed, have special needs, and are of color. These are the ones who remain on the waiting lists. These children come with histories and difficulties that most of us feel aren't our problem to fix and hope someone else will take them in.

* * *

If you were to drive along Central and 33rd Streets in Indianapolis, you might just bump into a quiet gentleman wearing a baseball cap and checked flannels with paint and splinters under his nails, and coming out of Unleavened Bread. Chris Provence is an unassuming, yet dynamic character. He talks passionately and excitedly and thinks intently about everything you ask him before he molds an answer. Along with his wife Mary, he has gone on to do for Indianapolis what Habitat for Humanity is doing at large.

Chris and Mary's plan is straightforward. They buy abandoned houses from the local housing department and with teams of volunteers, fix the buildings up and sell them to low-income families that would otherwise never have the opportunity to own their own home. They do this not because they want to run a home ownership corporation, but because of the children who used to attend their Bible study group in the Reagan Park neighborhood.[23]

Having held the group for several years, Chris and Mary noticed a continual turnover in the children who attended, whose families were constantly on the move because rent and taxes kept being hiked up. At first the Provences had homeless children literally staying in their own home, making beds on sofas for a night or two until social services could provide a more fixed place. After they had their own children, they started to think up other ways they could contribute to long-term change in their neighborhood.

When we lived in Indianapolis we got to be part of one of their big customary housewarming parties for one family. Kendall played music while I sat and people watched. There was no pomp or ribbon cutting. They served hot dogs and juice and just enjoyed friends and family, new neighbors and volunteers getting together to celebrate this huge milestone. I remember when they gave the mom the key to her house, she squealed and cried and talked breathlessly. I remember her two daughters, who were wearing spring-colored dresses and running round and round with other excited children through the rooms of their brand new home.

* * *

It's quite straightforward to think of Colombian street kids and children growing up in America's poorest zip codes as the "least of these" about whom Jesus spoke. But when I scratch the surface a little harder, I see there is need among others who are a little older, who live in lovely houses, and go to good schools. There are those who endure the silent and oppressive nature of depression until it spills out in addiction, self-harm and more desperately—suicide.

World Health Organization has estimated that around 121 million people worldwide suffer from depression; twenty-one million of those live in the U.S.[24] Between 20 percent and 50 percent of teens who suffer from depression already have this same problem in their family history. In an ongoing climate of economic uncertainty and its slow improvement, it's not difficult to see why this is so. And yet more damaging, two-thirds of sufferers will never seek treatment, which in turn leads to suicide, the third leading cause of death among teenagers.[25]

For others, eating disorders like anorexia or bulimia are their silent torment. There are an estimated ten million sufferers of eating disorders in the States.[26] One in 200 American women suffer from anorexia, while two to three in 200 suffer from bulimia. Ten to fifteen percent of anorexia or bulimia sufferers are male, and it is the third most common chronic illness among adolescents. More people die from anorexia than depression, between 5 percent and 10 percent of anorexics will die within ten years of being diagnosed, and still less than 45 percent seek treatment or go to general medical doctors rather than specialists for help.[27] Sometimes they do go to a specialist for treatment but are sent home dangerously early.

These figures are shocking yet unsurprising in our society full of conflicting messages about image and self-worth. Earlier this year, a London newspaper interviewed Kenneth Tong, a man who used Twitter to encourage young women to "get thin, or die trying."[28] He, of course, did it for the notoriety, but the fact is hundreds of girls still signed up to follow his messages of hate and starvation.

I think about my own attitude and hesitation to include these "Western issues" in with the other despairing ones from around the world. In some way depression and all its friends may seem to pale in comparison to eight-year-olds sleeping on concrete under bits of plastic or homeless low-income American children, but therein lies the problem. Issues are not always grand or obvious. They can be quiet, stealthy, and unassuming, but they still need to be addressed.

* * *

Jesus liked children. We're told only a little bit about his interaction with those younger ones who were around at the time, but what he did say about them and how he treated them spoke volumes. A well-known episode with Jesus, his disciples, and some local children comes to mind:

> Let the little children come to me, and do not hinder them, for the kingdom of God belongs to such as these. I tell you the truth, anyone who will not receive the kingdom of God like a little child will never enter it. (Mark 10:14-15)

We learn not only that we can understand God better if we're open and trusting like children, but that Jesus simply wanted to spend some time surrounded by them. Previously, he had been talking about highbrow issues of rank and status, sin and divorce; now he just wanted theology-free company. Perhaps it is in this moment we see something tender and uncomplicated. We see Jesus embracing children, though we never find out exactly what they were speaking about. We see him love them, defend their importance and relevance. We see a pattern laid out for ourselves.

When my friend Ericka went to Colombia, she met Rosie, a Colombian woman in her early forties who had spent years befriending and visiting the street kids of Medellín. Ericka remembers one afternoon the most clearly. A small child Rosie had never seen before walked towards them, his eyes glazed from sniffing glue, his clothes matted and stinking, and his hair filled with lice. Instead of stepping around the eight-year-old, Rosie called him "mi amor" and gave him the tightest hug he had probably received in a while. Rosie loved and still loves those children as though they are her own. She doesn't see the filthy hair and fingernails. She calls them her precious ones and holds their cheeks, like an aunt would. And they don't run away—maybe because of shock or maybe because she's a reminder of love.

I see that whether we're in our home country or living or volunteering abroad somewhere, children's and teenagers' needs are the same everywhere: to be held, known, and blessed. They will always remain the most vulnerable among us and will need us to acknowledge their existence. Part of seeing poverty doesn't just mean having pity or compassion; it means being affected to the point where we are fixated on how we can be part of making it right.

Be a kid again

Volunteer at your local afterschool care center. This will give you the opportunity to have such rewarding experiences as flying kites, playing with Legos, swinging on the swing set (I don't care how old you are, swings are still very cool!), reading Dr. Seuss again, and playing on the merry-go-round until you feel sick—the absolute best parts of being a child. Every major city has these types of centers. Visit http://www.afterschoolalliance.org to find where the afterschool programs are in your state.

Go out to eat

Chances are there is a single mother or father within a couple blocks of your front door. Knock on their door and see if you can take them out. The best thing I remember from being a child was getting carryout and going to the local park.

Eat dinner outside and spend the evening playing with the kids.

Take kids to work

(Unless you work for a Crime Scene Investigation unit—but how many of you CSIs can actually be reading this?) If you don't have children of your own, take some nieces or nephews or borrow some from a neighbor. It's a really incredible phenomenon to see how you change whenever children are around. Your co-workers will start to see you as more human. It's also really hard to look professional (or grumpy, for that matter) while carrying around a stuffed Winnie the Pooh.

Sponsor a child

Yes, it is one of the most common forms of support that church groups deal out these days. But it is also still one of the most helpful and rewarding. If you or your group decides to do this, make sure you do your research. Don't let your donation get swallowed up in the organization's operating expenses. Also, all of these organizations have their own rules and policies. Make sure you read up on their websites before you make a decision.

Here are a few places to start:
http://cs.ncm.org
http://www.worldvision.org
http://www.compassion.com

Consider adoption

This is a heavy one, huh? Some of the suggestions in this book can be done in just a few seconds—others in a few minutes. This suggestion is on the complete opposite side of the spectrum. This one will change your entire life.

Adoption is a bit risky. You never know how your child will turn out. But according to my parents, you never know how your biological kids will turn out either. (I'm not too sure what they meant by that.) So it doesn't really matter all that much now, does it? Regardless, why not take the risk? There are so many children out there who do not have loving parents. Here's a huge way to give love.

Read up about it at:
http://adoption.state.gov
http://www.adopt.org

Talk to the children

Think back to when you were child: it was a bit rough at times, wasn't it? Even the best parents ignore their children at times. Have a conversation with some six-, seven-, or eight-year-old while you and their parents are all stuck in an elevator somewhere. The child's parents most likely won't even think it's strange, and the things you hear will be some of the most interesting and funniest things you will hear that day. Promise.

Send some moolah

Streams of Mercy is an organization that is doing very good things for the street children in Bogotá. Many of their workers are volunteers, so your money gets to the people who need it most instead of being spent entirely on administration costs.

Get involved at:
http://www.streamsofmercy.org/about.htm

5
RECONSTRUCTED BB GUNS *and* AK-47s

"Our lives begin to end the day we become silent about things that matter."

—MARTIN LUTHER KING, JR.[1]

A machine hammers a single sheet of metal until it makes a small, brass bullet. The bullet rolls along the machinery belt and is picked up and inspected. The bullet is placed with others and checked again by a Ukrainian soldier before being packed onto a ship. The container is opened again in West Africa and is carried on the back of a pickup truck among a group of armed men. The bullet is picked up, loaded in a firearm, and fired—straight into the head of a thirteen-year-old boy.²

So begins the 2005 film *Lord of War*. The rest of the film chronicles the international work of Nicolas Cage's character, Yuri, as he becomes an arms dealer to meet the demand of providing firearms. But the film goes beyond the simplistic and into the largely undiscussed foray of weapons and their unruly power over and effect on us.

We barely have to skim our online newspapers or radio news sound bites before we learn about wars, threats of wars, suicide bombings, friendly fire, drive-by shootings, high school killings, and gang warfare. We see guns in plenty of popular movies; in fact, the better the special effects explosions, the more tweets the film may get. We see them in TV shows and in video games, where we can be the armed combatants.³ The game *Call of Duty: Modern Warfare 2* did this so well its makers faced criticism from both war veterans and the families of soldiers. War conflict video games have grown so popular that this particular one sold five million copies on its release date, totalling $310 million in twenty-four hours.⁴ By January 2010, the company had had made $1 billion.

The games are slick and are designed to look like the real thing. When you start the scenario with your avatar soldier, you are immersed in a world that looks exactly like Afghanistan, with dust, locals, and the native tongue of the enemy being spoken. You have a team and a mission, but better yet, you have a powerful and cleverly created weapon that will kill your enemy on the spot. You can even swap places and become one of the opposing forces and shoot at American soldiers.[5]

It is the crisp realism that makes these games so popular, but it is also what has offended both AMVETS and Massachusetts' Gold Star Families, among other groups. For those who have lost family members in the recent wars, the rise of these games must be confusing and heartbreaking at the same time. And yet we're fascinated and thrilled by having control of some virtual arms and being involved in virtual fights that closely resemble the real ones happening everywhere. We seem to like guns.

Guns and all that is connected to them have become ingrained in our society in the same way technology and social media are. They are seen as the norm rather than the exception and are part of life as we know it. The question of arms is old stomping ground in the States; the Second Amendment saw to that. They are a part of history, culture, security, and for many have nothing to do with the heinous war crimes that have seen Charles G. Taylor, the former President of Liberia, on trial for fueling atrocities in Sierra Leone.

As unrelated as the firearms in the recent Tucson, Arizona, shooting seem to those used in Kono, Sierra Leone, during the civil war, the results of these small arms are identical. Most of us assume and connect the world's greatest wars and their sins with tanks, bomber jets, or submarines, but the truth is it is the pistols, handguns, and submachine guns that do the most damage as they are cheap, easily accessible, and portable.[6] I learned that not only does this mean small arms are perfect for illicit trafficking, but they are also simple and small enough for children to operate.

There are approximately 300,000 child soldiers in the world.[7] Although Africa's child soldiers have become common knowledge due to movies like *Lord of War* and the scores of non-profit organizations working on the ground, it is Asia that has the single highest number of warring children. Burma has the highest number of child soldiers, with 75,000 being trained and kept in the country's deepest jungles.[8] Burma's long-standing ethnic divisions and competition have meant that a number of groups, from the Democratic Karen Buddhist Army (DKBA) to the Karenni National People's Liberation Front (KNPLF), have taken to using children as soldiers.[9] But perhaps more disturbing is that it's the State Peace Development Council, or Burma's national army, that "recruits" the most children.

It's not difficult to understand why Marcus Young began Project: AK-47 to take on the daunting task of finding and rescuing as many of those boys and girls as he and his team could. Six years later they are still calling for freedom, negotiating with the Burmese government to release the children, and running restoration homes to give the children who are demobilized a tangible afterlife. They work with partners and local volunteers who serve as house parents and counselors, teachers and guardians. They have sponsorship programs to make education a possibility again and a 200-acre farm for those who want to inherit five acres to be able to provide for their family. They do all of this for little ones like Sanan, who was sold to the army by his uncle when he was nine years old.

109

On his first day, he was gang raped by the other boy soldiers, under the watch of the "boss" (another older child soldier), then sent to collect bottles and cans that could be recycled or resold. That was his first day. Every day after was spent being a personal slave, keeping watch, collecting firewood, training, and when allowed, sleeping without a blanket in the frigid night winds. Project: AK-47 rescued him when he was eleven years old. He now lives in one of the rehabilitation houses and is back at school where he hopes to learn a lot to help "his people and guarantee a better life for them."[10]

Michael Oyella's story is a little different, and yet the same. When he was nine years old he was kidnapped in a raid by the Lord's Resistance Army (LRA) in Kitgum, Uganda. He witnessed the beheading of his seven-year-old brother when the little boy told his captors he was tired from the long hike to the border of Sudan. He was trapped in the LRA for seven years. He was trained and brainwashed to kill and fight, to ambush and torture. He became a "husband" to the female Lieutenant Atto and suffered humiliations he still won't talk about. When he escaped, he hid in a hut in Amira's (a small town in Acholi land, north Uganda) Internally Displaced People's (IDP) camp.

He calls his escape "luck from God" because he was able to slip between the Ugandan and LRA's crossfire and finally made his way to Kicuw's (another small town in Acholi land, north Uganda) reception center. It was there he began his slow rehabilitation process. It was also there he met the boys who killed his brother. I remember expecting to hear anger in his voice and a demand for revenge, but I heard neither. To Michael, they were all child soldiers being forced to kill—there was no difference.

Guns and children is a phenomenon found a lot closer to home too. A British actor named Ross Kemp made a documentary series called *Ross Kemp on Gangs*, which explored the effects of gang violence on countries around the world. His episode "Ross Kemp on Gangs: USA" put a magnifying glass on arms in the States. Kemp went to St. Louis, Missouri, one of the five most violent cities in the US, and spoke to mourning families, girlfriends, the local police and even gang members while they toyed with loaded guns.[11]

The episode starts off in Walnut Park, an inner-city neighborhood, where Kemp meets the mother, grandmother, and sister of a seventeen-year-old boy named Robert Walker. Robert was killed on May 5, 2006, when he got off his school bus with his cousin. He was shot six times from his head to legs. It's disturbing partly because he was so young and that so little was done to find the killers, but mostly because of what his mother says about no one caring when a child in their area is shot "because that's what they do—shoot each other."

It shouldn't matter that this mother is a single parent, African-American, and in a low-paying job. It shouldn't matter that when she speaks she uses slightly different words to make her point. All that should matter is that she's grief stricken, that her only son is dead and she is no closer to justice than she was on the afternoon he was shot. But most won't get past the neighborhood where she lives and the things that happen there because they don't go there. Some don't even know where her neighborhood is in their city.

Whether I was in Nashville, Indianapolis, Chicago, or Los Angeles, separation among people was apparent, even after all these years. We eat in the same restaurants and shop in the same grocery stores. We use the same libraries and work for the same companies. We live together now, but in so very many ways, we don't. Maybe most of these gaps are due more to socioeconomic differences than the prickly race issue, but the point still stands that we're divided. Though things have changed in legislation and rights, too often there's still awkwardness, or alienation between different ethnic groups. The relationships are still strained.

There was a video going around Facebook and YouTube for a while that had everyone who heard it mimicking the young man on camera. It was a news report about a woman whose house was broken into and how the burglar tried to climb into her bed. Her brother was there and fought off the intruder. When he told the news reporter this story, he became very animated, except it wasn't clear if he was joking or serious when he said, "Hide yo' wife, hide yo' kids and hide yo' husband too becos they's rapin' ervbody up in here." This one line is the reason the video became viral; it's the line that has been mimicked and laughed at countless times by its viewers. It's also the line and our response to it that cries so much more of that yawning gap between us.

The tragedy is how we've used our neighborhood, city, and county lines to mark our territories. We withdraw into our safe zones and what's familiar until what's different only becomes more different and more difficult to relate to. Until we can't understand, can't appreciate, don't fully get involved in what it must be like to live in a place where seventeen-year-olds are shooting each other. Gang culture (its violence, in particular) is not a new topic. It's been discussed and picked apart, studied and turned into films, but it's also slipped into a social tragedy that most of us want to be as far away from as possible.

There are several gangs in St. Louis, the largest two being the Bloods and the Crips. Some say they're copycats of the L.A. gangs, others that they're real and brought the unforgiving drug trade to St. Louis in the 1990s. Either way, they are filled with children. It's estimated that every two weeks a child dies in St. Louis, and plenty of teddy-bear-covered trees mark their deaths.[12] The streets look like battlegrounds with bullet holes and gang names tagged on walls and on the sidewalks. A radio presenter in Ross Kemp's documentary distills what's happening into "kids killing kids."[13] I wonder where these kids even get the guns, and I learn they may be received, stolen, or bought for protection.

When I read more on the prevalence of and access to guns, I find public opinions that leave me wondering how this great divide became so entrenched. Some comments that hit the hardest are the ones that blame gun crimes solely on African-Americans and Mexicans or the comments like "if any hood rat or welfare mother had a baby they should imprison the baby to prevent future crimes."[14] There is no denying the disconnect, the chasm that divides us even though we're living in the same city, in the same district, in the same country with the same basic needs. It's us and them, here and there. How many times have we thought of gang violence as the bearer's fault rather than the gun's? How many of us have blamed the ills of crime and social breakdown on these "others?" How many of us have uttered the phrase: "Those who live by the sword . . . ?"

In January of 2008, Jireh Sports merged with Shepherd Community Center and moved to Shepherd's facility on East Washington Street in Indianapolis. Shepherd works in a low-income neighborhood and provides food, clothing, a health clinic, mental and spiritual guidance and tutoring, job skills and even college mentoring to those who live nearby. They work with the marginalized, the ones we don't notice unless we know them personally. And they've done so well that even the Indianapolis Colts football team is joining their efforts.[15]

But it's Tim Streett's story, the founder of Jireh Sports, that most captures me. It reads like a twenty-first century parable in its tragedy and redemption. Tim started Jireh Sports to live among those whose poverty is harsh, where windows are boarded up in derelict homes and the grass grows too high. In 1978, when he was fifteen years old, his father was shot in the head in an armed robbery while he and his father were shoveling snow in their driveway. Tim was left to live, grieve, and spiral downward, wandering around lost until it dawned on him that the boys who killed his father were many things, but mostly they were the urban poor.

After that he became fixed on one thing—racial reconciliation. He didn't want to just preach about the long-fraught tensions between people groups in America; he wanted to be part of the change. And so he wrote letters to the men who killed his father—one was serving a ninety-year sentence while another was on death row—to tell them he had forgiven them. But he didn't stop there; he befriended one of the men and went on to visit him in prison and build up a friendship. He worked with the case's prosecutor to see the sentence reduced from ninety years to twenty-three years. The man was freed in 2001 and now works as an auto mechanic.

Tim's story shakes us because he lived out Jesus' words of mercy. He went to prison to visit a man who was part of the armed robbery that ended his father's life. He became a friend to the lonely and a defender of the lowly. None of this is to say we're meant to be saints, but we do need to try to understand, to go behind the crime to see the homes and families that have released so many broken, hurt, and struggling people outside.

When I lived in Nashville, I had no idea that the farther up Gallatin Pike I drove, the further into the "ghetto" I went. People used (and still use) that word with an odd mixture of fear and bravado that they had to go only a few blocks and they would be in the thick of it. I heard of shootings and car chases. I was told I had to be cautious and should stay in my car whenever possible. But when I would drive down Gallatin, I just saw people living their lives. Sometimes they would jaywalk in front of my car or strike up conversations at the neighborhood Wal-Mart, but they were just lower income people living their lives. Maybe the real problems of drugs and prostitution are more prevalent on smaller streets rather than the main roads. Maybe the bad things that do happen, happen at night, but how does creating a bogeyman out of an entire area help us connect or help us stay together?

It seems Tim asked himself similar questions because he moved his family from a middle class setting to be among those he wanted to minister to, and he started Jireh Sports. I visited Jireh Sports a few years ago, before it merged with Shepherd Community Center, and I was able to walk around the facility. I remember seeing computer rooms, the gym, the squealing children, and a huge room full of school supplies that were ready for the children's new school year. I remember thinking that it wasn't saintly ministry pushing Tim to work, but a

115

strong hope for and belief in the children who lived in poverty, who were locked into generations of poverty.

Tim talks about generational poverty being its own culture just as much as the middle class and old money are distinct cultures. He talks of generations of families living below the poverty line. He talks about how they're able to stop the cycle only when individuals choose differently, are presented with an opportunity, or participate in an activity that causes them to believe they can break out of the cycle.

Tim recalls a boy named Corey who became part of Jireh Sports during his junior year of high school. He was a brilliant gymnast but was a little too old to enter the competitive level. The staff at Jireh still encouraged him to take up a sport, so he chose diving. A year or so later Corey won the Indiana State Championship, the first Indiana public school system student to do so since the 1950s and the first African-American ever. But with a family riddled with poverty, he was barely encouraged by his family and friends to continue education and dropped out of college in the middle of his freshman year. He tried again, later on, but quit within the first week, and he now has two children to look after.

Corey's story isn't unusual. In fact, it's so widespread that some commentators fear that by dropping out of high school and keeping only low-paying jobs individuals like Corey will single-handedly ruin America's future chances as a global power, which equates to an outsourcing of American jobs to Chinese and Indian graduates. However, when we look at the United States's future on this grand scale and in these terms, we miss knowing who these individuals like Corey are; we fail to appreciate that they might actually want a different life with a future for themselves and their children too.

Tim calls what's happening the "tyranny of the urgent." When you're financially, emotionally, and relationally stable, you tend to focus on your tomorrows. You think about increasing your savings so you can take two vacations instead of one. You think about what car you'll get next when this one has had enough years on it. You decorate and landscape your house because it means you'll get more for it when you want to sell it to buy a bigger one to display and store all the stuff you've acquired over the years. You encourage your children's education because it ensures a bright future for them. You save and invest for your retirement—and maybe a trip to Europe.

These middle class decisions and desires have become the norm for most of us, but if you're stuck in a cycle of generational poverty, the money you have is limited. It's not for the future; it's for now. You spend time working out how you will make it through this week when, once again, your needs and expenses are greater than the funds you have to cover it all. You live in each moment because you're not sure what the next one will bring. You buy food with questionable nutritious value because it's cheap and will suffice to keep the hunger pangs at bay. You send your children to school because they get a free meal there, and it serves as a day care that allows you to work. You plan where you might move if you're evicted, and TV is one of your few pleasures.[16]

To grow up living in the moment in the same way your parents and grandparents did creates a mold that is difficult to break. But even in these harsh and severe situations there is a flicker of something different. Jireh Sports calls it "a future story"—something they try to instill in all the children. They don't promise that all the kids will go on to play professional sports but that their future can be better than their today. There's the idea that their future can be promising with high school graduation and college, that they can achieve a new kind of future through relationships, role models, and support systems that tell them they haven't been overlooked and that they are important. They teach children to have a hope in their future. Without hope there will be gangs, drugs, and other temptations. I believe them when they say children don't join gangs because they want to be criminals but because they're looking for understanding and a place to belong.

There is hope, but there is also a cutting reality facing these children. Tim speaks of children who grow up aware that the world sees them merely as poor, black, the ones who go to public school, the ones who live on the wrong side of the tracks, the ones who aren't as special as other kids. He speaks of overcoming these limits, which when I see how deeply they run, honestly sounds like the most difficult thing to do, and I realize we all bear a responsibility in this. Perhaps we haven't ever said anything derogatory or prejudiced, but perhaps we simply haven't thought about them at all. We don't *see* them because we never cross paths until we read about shootings and deaths that make it into the news.

* * *

In the Old Testament God doesn't shy away from war. He uses it several times to demonstrate to Israel why he is the one true God. However, there are some unbelievably violent stories in which babies are killed, daughters of enemies are taken as concubines, and cities are plundered. And God is there all along. I am left wondering how a God of peace can ever be reconciled with so much bloodshed—until I remember I need the whole picture. The Bible is one gigantic story of humanity and our God. Who God is in the Old Testament cannot make complete sense without who God is in the New Testament.

Jesus fills in the picture of who God is—a God who loves all of his creation and wants to see us thrive. A God who is saddened by war and injustices and wants us to love each other as we claim to love him. Jesus certainly wasn't surprised by wars. He tells us, "You will hear of wars and rumors of wars, but see to it that you are not alarmed" (Matthew 24:6). But he didn't mean we should be apathetic to what's happening around us. Instead he tells us to turn the teaching of revenge into one of peace—that we should take the insult rather than strike back (see Matthew 5:38-39). It's easy to think Jesus' advice here is a bit too idealistic for the time we live in now—a time of revolutions, drug cartels, and terrorism. But to dismiss these words would be to miss the rest of what he means.

I don't think Jesus wanted us to be defenseless against those who hurt us, but instead, to change the whole mindset of how to deal with things when they go wrong—to set a different standard. Maybe even to lead the way into habits and practices that will save lives in the end. Jesus told us to turn our love for our neighbors into a love that can also include our enemies (see Matthew 5:43-44). He spoke of a love that doesn't lash out or avenge or demand a return of affection or service, but will keep on giving, over and over again. Peter talks about the same peace where we bless when we've been insulted or hurt. He goes even further by suggesting that people aren't usually harmed for doing good and that even if we are we shouldn't be afraid (see 1 Peter 3:9-14).

These are incredibly high demands, but when I consider that over 740,000 people die annually from armed violence,[17] millions are forced to migrate to displacement or refugee camps to survive the torture, abuse and death, or that the five permanent members of the UN security council (U.K., U.S.A, Russia, France, and China) are also the world's biggest arms exporters, I know these demands make sense.[18] We live in a world that, whether we think of it or not, is connected. We may use guns for different reasons—for self-defense, protection, or war—but the damage they cause is the same regardless of our intentions. There's an old quote that says, "guns don't kill people; people kill people," but the simple fact is guns make it a lot easier. They make human life expendable.

Lord of War ends with Yuri firmly believing that what other countries do with the guns he sold them isn't his problem. He continues with a play on scripture, saying, "the arms dealer will inherit the earth." But in April 2008 a group of South African church leaders, trade unions, and lawyers banded together to prevent a Chinese arms ship from docking in Durban to then send the rockets, grenades, and mortars bombs on board to Zimbabwe.[19] Despite the fact that the South African government had given the ship a transit license, this group blocked it. Mozambique and Namibia followed suit and prevented the arms from entering Africa through their ports. The ship managed to get rid of some goods in Luanda, Angola, before sailing back to China.[20]

If you're like me, you cheered when you read this story— because these groups of individuals wanted peace more than anything else. It's a story that gives us hope that violence doesn't always win and that maybe the arms dealer doesn't inherit the earth after all. The arms and gun trade is a difficult topic because it's so personal and asks so much of us. And I wonder if by having guns, we are hemming ourselves in from outside. Wanting safety is no bad thing, but perhaps the call is really to desire peace and a future for everyone.

Contact Congress

Cliché? Maybe a bit, but this is important, so stay with me. You remember old Westerns with John Wayne? He always carried a pistol and wore a really sweet hat. Imagine if somebody met up with the "other guys," the ones fighting John Wayne, and gave them rocket launchers (which weren't even invented then). The movies would have turned out differently. This is what's going on in developing countries. Developed countries (such as the one you're probably a citizen of) are providing arms to the bad guys. Please call or send a letter or an email to your government representative and demand that your country stop providing arms to rebel movements in foreign countries.

Stay informed

Don't put all your trust in one news source. Remember that they too are businesses and are just as interested in making money as your local gas station. Check several different news sources to balance the information you hear. Neither Fox News, CNN, CNBC, BBC, nor even Al Jazeera is right all the time (nor are any of them wrong all the time).

Provide a Saturday job

Driveway covered in snow? Grass a foot high? Yard buried in leaves? Why not ask one of the children from the neighborhood to take care of it? You'll have more time to do what you want to do, you'll be giving them some spending money, and who knows? They might just do a good job! Even if they don't, you will have given them something to do for a couple of hours that has kept them away from the television, video games, or any bad influences that might roam your neighborhood. Good work!

Adopt a family

Have them over for dinner periodically and see to it they're provided with a good, nutritious meal. Share stories and movies with them. See if you can find something you're all interested in.

Lock it up

If you feel it's necessary to own a firearm, please see to it that it is unloaded and locked securely in a cabinet—preferably with a trigger lock on it as well. Guns are inviting toys for children, and it's best to save their first experience for when they're old enough to handle them.

Be a mentor

Big Brothers Big Sisters is a very well-known mentoring program. They are always looking for volunteers, and it can be a very rewarding experience. If you were a real big brother or big sister at one point, remember how inspiring and encouraging you were to your younger siblings? Yeah, that's what I thought . . . This is your chance to redeem yourself for all those years you beat up on your younger siblings.

Go to:
http://www.bbbs.org to learn more about becoming a Big.

Tell people about child soldiers

Many of you have probably seen *Invisible Children* and know about child soldiers in Uganda. If you haven't, please watch it, as well as the other documentaries this organization has created.

The film focuses on the LRA (Lord's Resistance Army) who, after having abducted over 30,000 children in the last twenty years (http://kabiza.com/Lira-Children-Kony-Rebels.htm), have now finally retreated into the Democratic Republic of Congo.

However, to date, over twice that many children have been abducted in Burma. Project AK-47 is an organization that is committed to rescuing child soldiers all over the world. Drop by http://www.projectak47.com or http://www.invisiblechildren.com and read up on child soldiers; then share what you find with your friends and family.

6
the SICK NEED THE DOCTOR

Jesus' sacrifice was the epitome of something for nothing.

When Jesus called Matthew to join him, he did it over dinner with a crowd of people so dubious, the religious leaders of the day hovered outside grumbling about it (see Mark 2:13-16). His response was short, punchy, and as honest as Jesus always was: "It is not the healthy who need a doctor, but the sick" (Mark 2:17). It is commonly understood that Jesus was speaking about spiritual sickness and a person's soul, but just a quick look at his three years of ministry shows he meant his words literally too.

Jesus's concern for the poor and sick is apparent throughout the Gospels. He wasn't facing mild cases of measles or chickenpox but diseases that terrified everyone else and exiled their victims. There's the story of the man with leprosy who walks between the large crowds one day to kneel before Jesus to request what no one else could or would care to do: he asks Jesus to make him clean.

The people around would have pulled away from the stench and sight of his rotting flesh. They would have shouted at him for getting close instead of remaining on the edge and shouting, "unclean, unclean." And yet, true to his form, Jesus simply reaches out, touches him, assures him he wants to heal him, and tells him to follow the customs to confirm he's been healed (see Matthew 8:1-4). We don't hear what the man says when he gets his new skin, but the miracle is beyond even that. By reaching out his hand, Jesus shows his audience that this man is an ordinary person and worthy to be treated as such. He brings the man's position back from cursed to loved.

The bleeding woman shows us all over again how involved God is in our sufferings. Her illness seems more awkward and mysterious than leprosy. No one specifies why or how she was bleeding, just that it has been going on for twelve years. For twelve years she would have been shunned from the synagogue and community. She would have been alone as the village pariah. We're not told why God allowed her pain to go on so long. All we see is she too fights the crowd to reach out and touch Jesus—and she too is healed (see Luke 8:42-48).

These stories have been retold so many times they're Bible classics, but the urgent need of the sick and vulnerable in these stories is no different from so many who live around us now. If you talk to someone about wanting to be involved in rehabilitating drug-addicted former child soldiers or street kids, you will most likely receive a positive response. If you ask to be sponsored for a 5k run to raise money for cancer or Alzheimer's disease research, many will want to get involved. But, if you ask if anyone would be willing to sit with someone who is suffering neuropathic pain because their HIV is developing into AIDS, the responses may cool off.[1]

HIV and AIDS scare us like little else. They crept in in the 1980s and have stuck around to see around thirty-three million people around the world die of HIV-related causes.[2] There are currently more than one million people living with HIV in the U.S.[3] Around 1.1 million have AIDS, both children and adults alike.[4] Halting and reversing HIV/AIDS has also become one of the UN's key MDG goals to reach by 2015.[5]

Perhaps we're afraid because the illnesses are so drawn out, with painful health complications. Maybe it's the fear of catching the silent killer that is HIV, which has none of the nobleness of cancer or leukemia. Or perhaps it's because of how the illnesses can be transmitted (though not the only ways)—intravenous drugs or risky sex. For some reason, HIV and AIDS bring out opinions, judgments, and stigma that leave patients isolated and horribly alone.

Androsi Furaha is a wife, mother, sister, and daughter. She was raped by the FARDC (Forces Armées de la République Démocratique du Congo), the Democratic Republic of Congo's army. She and several other women and children were caught fleeing on the road from Chekele and were gang raped and left with HIV. She is now in the terminal stages of AIDS.

In the DRC, if a woman is raped, it is seen as an embarrassment to the family, tribe, and victim's husband. She is seen as a disgrace. If she gets pregnant or contracts HIV, her family and community disown her. There are estimated to be around 10,000 girls and women in DRC who are infected with HIV or AIDS.[6] These women have been left to live with the trauma, shame, loss, economic and social downturn, as well as the medical complications. Only through small, self-organized support groups and church projects have these women been able to start the rehabilitation process.

A woman named Cey in Kenya was infected by her fiancé. He disappeared, married someone else, and left her to face the task of telling her parents the news alone. She's not on medication and doesn't ask for assistance. Instead she asks for someone to share this time with—a life partner.[7]

There's something about human company that's integral to who we are. We're born from a couple and into a family. We have ancestors and relatives. Sometimes we even have extended families and friends who are like family. Having people around us when we're ill isn't just comfort—it is a lifesaver. This is especially true of HIV and AIDS patients, who oftentimes enter into chronic depression after hearing the news "HIV positive."[8] Despite improved antiretroviral drugs and more medical knowledge about the virus, the stigma, discrimination, and discomfort surrounding it make it hard to fight without the emotional support of others.

Dr. Denis Mukwege understands just how much "others" are part of the healing from his work with Congolese women. Since the war began in 1998, he has helped as a surgeon, midwife, friend, and protector and is now part of the City of Joy Center, which has just recently opened as a refuge for these women. The center will serve 180 women between the ages of fourteen and fifty. It will be a place where they can be part of group therapy, use storytelling, dance, and theatre for their own stories. A place where they can learn horticulture, ecology, and self-defense. A place where they aren't simply victims, but women being restored with dignity and hope. And as the war continues to rage on Congo's eastern border with Uganda, where scores of women are still raped every day and run the risk of infection, this center's promise of joy has never been more needed.

Sub-Saharan Africa has long been the worst-hit victim, with 22.5 million people living with HIV or AIDS. In 2009, 1.3 million died from AIDS and 1.8 million people became infected with HIV. Since HIV and AIDS first arrived, 14.8 million children have lost one or both their parents to the diseases.[9]

I was still quite young when it started becoming clear to people that what was happening in Africa was an epidemic. We lived in London, so it seemed like a distant problem, but I remember my Aunty Susan. She wasn't really my aunt; she was my mom's best friend, and she was dying from AIDS. At first they never told us why she was losing so much weight, even though we would go to visit. Toward the end, when she was bedridden at home, they let us go into her room to see her properly.

My Aunty Susan had always been a strong, slim lady. She was always the one at family parties dancing when everyone else had taken off their shoes, but the person in her bed looked nothing like her. There's a reason people used to call HIV and AIDS the wasting disease. She was tiny, just a fraction of what she used to be. She had gone blind, and her hearing was starting to go too. I'm not sure if there is ever a good age to see someone die of AIDS-related illnesses, but I'm glad we did, as she died in the early hours the next morning.

In my first week at Naggalama, Uganda, Elijah, one of the other children's counselors, took me on some home visits down into one of the villages that is so off the beaten track I would have been lost for days had I tried to make the journey alone. The woman we went to see was lying on a bed in a dimly lit room that had in it only some woven mats, sandals, a calendar, and a couple of pots. Even from where I was standing, I could see she was incredibly frail under the covers.

There was another lady there with her—a neighbor who had come to make her some lunch and sit with her. This neighbor had no medicine or medical expertise, just an unyielding love for her friend. And now I see that justice was being served to this dying woman who was made ill by her deceased husband.

I see that if we can give of our time and make such hard times more bearable, maybe we're helping to right a grievous wrong.

In most parts of sub-Saharan Africa, grandmothers have become mothers all over again. Not because they want to relive motherhood, but because their sons and daughters and spouses have died from AIDS. The effect of losing working parents is crushing and is still being seen and felt all over. The family income drops immediately, which can mean a huge loss in clothing, food, shelter, education, and health. Children have to grow up quickly and raise their siblings or take over all the chores. They may have to beg or turn to prostitution to raise money.

It's a strange thing to be in a country and see that a whole generation of people from their mid-twenties to forties is missing. But you do see it. You see it in the teenage girl who is walking miles and carrying heavy water bottles back from the well for home. You see it in the little boy who is riding a bicycle that is so big for him he has to slip through the bicycle frame and pedal because his feet won't reach the pedals if he uses the seat. And you see it in the tired face of the old woman who's covered her head with a headscarf in the hot sun.

There is a time when Jesus returns to Capernaum after traveling through Galilee. He is in Peter's house and there are lots of people there to hear him talk. The house is so crowded they can't stand outside the door, but four friends are determined to get their friend to Jesus. They dig a hole in the roof and lower him into the middle of the room, right in front of Jesus. The Bible says he saw their faith and then spoke to the paralytic. *He saw their faith.* He saw their stubborn refusal to lose this opportunity. He saw their determination to be with their friend through his situation and fight for him any way they could.

* * *

If anyone had told me a few years ago that water could be just as deadly a killer as HIV and AIDS, I would have started listing its life-saving properties. However, water isn't just our elixir of life; it's a carrier of disease. Every year 1.4 million children die from waterborne diseases, while 70 percent of the world's freshwater supply is used on agriculture.[10]

Seth Maxwell is a twenty-two-year-old L.A. film student turned world-saver. Katie Basbagill is a photographer with a heart and eyes that see and feel everything. Together they went with seven others to Swaziland, a small landlocked country, with the Thirst Project. They went to continue the mammoth task of raising $40 million to see that Swaziland's 1.1 million people have clean, safe water.

When I ask why they would take on such a huge job, Seth tells me about a conversation he had with a World Vision worker. In a country that is the size of New Jersey, 25.9 percent of the adult population (between ages fifteen and forty-nine) are HIV positive.[11] Being HIV-infected means their immune systems have or will become so weak that the likelihood they will die quite quickly from drinking dirty water increases astronomically.

It's hard to imagine safe water being so scant, but when we learn that scientists have estimated that by 2025, 800 million people will be living in countries or regions with absolute water scarcity,[12] the reality becomes more apparent. But even before 2025, so much is already happening around us telling us there's a water problem. Less than 3 percent of the world's water supply is freshwater; yet because of a lack of infrastructure, developing countries dump 70 percent of their untreated industrial waste into what would have been usable waters. One in six people do not have access to safe freshwater.[13] Lack of safe water feeds into poor sanitation, which kills more people than wars. Two and a half billion people do not have a toilet or latrine or any way to hygienically separate human feces from human contact.[14] More than one billion people do not have any sanitation. The result has been the growth of aggressive and swift illnesses like diarrhea.

Diarrhea is the second biggest cause of death among children. Around 1.5 million children die from it every year. That is more than measles, AIDS, or malaria combined.[15] More plainly, every twenty seconds a child dies because of poor sanitation and preventable illnesses.[16] This is what our world looks like in places far away from us. This is how the majority of nameless, faceless individuals live. It's unlikely that we will go to the slums, shantytowns, and landfills with these people and know them by name, but that doesn't absolve us of the fact that these millions and billions are suffering. The refrain is loud and clear: everyone needs fair water distribution and a chance in this life.

It's this reality that keeps Seth and Katie fixed on a job that would deter so many others. Over the holidays they created a new way to tackle this goal—the $5 campaign. Seth's friend actor Michael Welch sent out requests via Twitter, Facebook, and YouTube to ask his fans and supporters to donate $5 to build a well in Swaziland and to rebuild an existing well in Uganda. If both well projects succeeded, he would take one participant, chosen at random, to join him and go to meet the people using the wells in Africa. Both goals were met and they'll be going out later this year to see the completed work.

* * *

God is very particular about infectious skin diseases. In the book of Leviticus, he goes into great detail about how to identify a sore, what the steps of examination are, and how to treat it (see chapters 14 and 15). It's so vivid and thorough, it's like reading a medical manual. He was speaking to Israel as they were adjusting to life outside of Egypt. They were living in tents and not houses, and they hadn't yet arrived in Canaan. Perhaps their bodies were still adjusting to all these new changes, or they were camped too close to each other, or they weren't being clean enough, which was causing them to develop new diseases their bodies weren't used to. Whatever the cause, God was concerned about them and was diagnosing and treating them as any doctor would.

There's a clinic in Kansas City that is run by a couple of doctors. This clinic has become a refuge of sorts to the people around it. Dr Lee and her co-doctor serve a neighborhood where the average earnings are around $11,000 per year and where unemployment is on the rise again. Her patients come from the lower-income working class, and a third of them live below the poverty line in an area that has all been but forgotten by its county. For these patients, getting seen by a doctor and having treatment are expenses that not many can afford to do. And with ever-increasing hospital costs, it's a real fear.[17]

A few years back, when I lived in Nashville, I went with a friend to a low-income neighborhood clinic. The idea of the clinic was to provide people with medical care at low or no cost. Some had Medicaid, while others had Medicare, but for others this one trip would mean the difference between how many and what kinds of meals their entire family would have for the rest of the month. It would mean the difference between paying all the bills or choosing the most important ones.

Out of around 330 million Americans, forty-six million of them will sit in clinics like these waiting for care. They'll wait there because insurance companies can refuse them for their pre-existing conditions or navigate sophisticated hidden clauses that protect them from paying out when help is needed. And I wonder how we have gotten to the point that we will try to avoid helping the very least of these. How we'll label them as lazy and uncommitted to finding work and declare, as some self-proclaimed Christian politicians have, that "people shouldn't get something for nothing." But I see that they're missing the point and missing God's method of dealing with people, with life, and with justice.

But Jesus' sacrifice was the epitome of something for nothing. It was everything for nothing. When he died, he pleaded that we would be forgiven in exchange for his life. When he lived he asked us to take care of the least of these. He spoke of being naked and someone clothing him. He spoke of being sick and someone looking after him. He spoke of being a prisoner and someone visiting him. And mostly, he told us when we did this, we were really doing it for him.

Sometimes it's hard to imagine Jesus as anything other than one standing in glowing robes, offering benediction, and being the champion of the victors. Yet, for most of his life, Jesus was with the outcasts and the downtrodden. Today he would be with the morbidly obese, the crack addict and the person dying from AIDS. When he tells us when we do these things we're doing it for him, maybe he's reminding us of their bottomless worth. True justice does not mean helping and then asking, What will I get in return? This justice wants to see others healthy, not because of a heavenly reward but because they were made in God's image. They look like him, just as we all do.

God's love was not just a spiritual, mystical experience that filled rooms with sweet fragrances and skies with clouds by day and fires by night. It was living and breathing, from Jesus, who touched decomposing skin, to the apostles, who went through streets and prayed for the sick (see Acts 5:12-16). Life for the apostles was tough. Not only were there natural illnesses and ailments going around; they were being hounded by Rome, beaten, and executed for spreading God's message. Nevertheless, they still sought to love and to give. They turned God's love for and commitment to them into an offering for others.

In Acts we learn that the apostles pooled their resources together so that no one would be without, no one would be lacking or without care. Undoubtedly some early Christians were richer than others and probably gave more, but they didn't see it as an injustice; rather, they were happy to be able to show others how Christ's love took care of everyone. The apostles weren't trying to be political or take sides in sharing their goods; they were simply exercising a needed human economy.

We spent $2.3 trillion on health care in 2008,[18] and yet some people struggled with diseases that ate away at their nervous systems and muscles because they couldn't afford a $200 blood test that would have determined they had Huntington's disease.[19] We spent $41 billion on our pets,[20] while others halved their diabetes medication to lower their bills even though they were left bedridden in the end. I love animals, especially dogs. Animals need our care too and need to be treated with kindness. But when we can spend billions on them while people suffer from life threatening diseases, I wonder at the balance of things and I wonder at our priorities.

Our reality is that some of us have more than enough and are free to do what we please with our excess. Others are managing to exist inside what was marked out in the 1948 Universal Declaration of Human Rights:

> Everyone has the right to a standard of living adequate for the health and well-being of himself and of his family, including food, clothing, housing and medical care and necessary social services, and the right to security in the event of unemployment, sickness, disability, widowhood, old age or other lack of livelihood in circumstances beyond his control.[21]

We all have the right to an adequate standard of living, but that isn't what we witness around the world. The question of how we choose to solve this is left open to us.

* * *

There's a widely known Bible scene that places Jesus by a well in Samaria, talking to a Samaritan woman and asking her for a drink (see John 4:1-26). It's a hot day. The notes in the concordance say it's about midday and the disciples had gone into town to get something for lunch. The woman—a reject in the community, whose name we are never given—is drawing water at a time when no one else would be in the blazing heat. Jesus asks her for a drink and then starts to talk to her, shattering everything she's ever known about Jews and affirming old prophesies.

There are a few odd and yet wonderful moments in this story, like when he talks about living water and she thinks he's found a new filtered stream. But one rings loudest of all. He recognizes her as somebody, and he sits with her. He discusses her past without judgment and hints at how much she's loved instead.

* * *

The human body is a work of art. It's everything like the psalmist says: "it is fearfully and wonderfully made." Every part of it is so intentional, from the tips of our tongues, which like our fingerprints have a unique mark, to our noses, which can recognize 50,000 scents. It's no wonder God was so specific in his guidelines for preserving our bodies: God was passionate in wanting to protect Israel's health and well-being. Perhaps these passages of the Bible should remind us when we forget just how precious every single one of us is.

It doesn't matter whether we are the six-year-old Bangladeshi boy whose slum home has no sanitation or the forty-year-old widow who was raped and left with HIV. Whether we're the sixty-eight-year-old man who's discovered he has Parkinson's disease and has lost his job because it required a steady hand and now has no health insurance, or whether we're ourselves and we're trying to steer through our own anxieties. We are precious—every single one.

Some of the needs we encounter are so deep and urgent and yet full of complexities that jostle our idea of what is right living and what is wrong. Some of these needs may be terminal, and we won't be able to fix them. But even with numbers stacked with tragedy and toil, we can still give the greatest offering we have—our ears, our hands, our love, and our time.

Precious

You can buy two bags of chips for under a dollar at some gas stations. Unfortunately, two bags of chips too often become an entire meal for children. People who don't understand nutrition aren't only in developing countries. Many times, they are right down the street.

It's a hard one to watch, but if you have a free evening it might be good to watch the film *Precious*. It provides an interesting look at American life below the poverty line.

Carry a reusable water bottle

Yeah, those plastic Aquativa bottles are handy, and how cool does it look to have hundreds of them stacked neatly in your refrigerator? However, the truth is that they are wreaking havoc on our environment.

In America alone around 2.5 million plastic bottles are used every hour, and most of them make their way into a landfill.

You can pick up a very green, BPA-free, reusable water bottle at any local sporting goods store for what you spend on a couple of lattes. Besides, aren't they just filling those disposable plastic bottles with tap water anyway?

Learn more recycling facts at:
http://www.recycling-revolution.com/recycling-facts.html
http://www.democracynow.org/2007/8/1/the_bottled_water_lie_as_soft

How to save some lives

CPR. It's not just for the suave doctors on *Grey's Anatomy*, *House*, *ER*, or, if you're really old school, *Chicago*.

Find a course to teach you what those three letters mean and commit what you learn to memory.

I hope you never have to use it, but feel happier knowing you're a bit more ready.

The Red Cross will point you in the right direction:
http://www.redcross.org

Water.loo

I couldn't resist, but don't worry; this page won't break out into Abba's rendition.

No, but seriously, there are places on earth in countries probably an eight-hour flight away that have no running water, no safe water to drink, or no way to stay healthy and hygienic.

In 2011, we're still dying of preventable waterborne diseases.

Get some friends together and pool your pennies, run a race, or have an auction, and build a family a loo (that's a toilet, for all you non-British readers) for $30.

Find out more here:
http://www.water.org
http://www.thirstproject.org

Flo Nightingale and Mary Seacole

Despite the ongoing debate surrounding the health care reform, good things are still being done.

Why not use Google maps to find out where the free/assisted health clinics (for low-income clients) are? Then choose one to stop by and see what they need.

Or better yet, find out the names of the staff and their position and ask them how you can help.

You'll be surprised.

Drop in

This one's difficult but so needed. Find out from your local hospital if any of the AIDS patients would like any visitors; if you get a yes, go and sit with them for a while.

Take a book, a puzzle, some knitting, or Sudoku and see what they want to do.

Then go back the next week, and the week after that.

7
ABCs *and* **TESOL**

"Your neighbor is the holiest object presented to your senses."

—C. S. LEWIS[1]

My friend Rachel told me a funny story the other day, and it still makes me giggle when I think about it. She and her husband Nate had just moved to Thailand to work with children, teaching them English, among other things. In Thailand, food is a very important part of everyday life, and most people greet each other with, "What did you have for lunch?" One day a group of Thai children asked her, "What did you eat with rice?" which is slang for the usual greeting. Seeing as she was still learning the language it sounded very close to, "Who did you eat with?" So Rachel answered, "Nate and Tawee." The children nearly burst laughing and spent every day after that reminding her, "You ate Nate!"

I love this story. It's short, simple, and full of the crossed wires that happen when cultures collide. But perhaps most of all it tells us something about language—its powers and fallibilities and its necessity to connect us all. It's our voice if others are to hear us. For the refugee, asylum seeker, orphan, street child, human trafficking victim, child soldier, or malaria patient, language is more than just communication; it is the difference between an education and a life lost in the many holes in our world.

I'm not just talking about local languages, but the one that has tied the world together even more tightly than the Internet— English. For many of us, English is our mother tongue. We learned it without thinking about why words are ordered the way they are or how much access and how many opportunities in life it gives us. English is the world's shared language. It's the *lingua franca* of trade, the working language, the common tongue we all use to understand each other. Around 328 million people speak English as their first language. There are 112 English-speaking countries in the world, and around 600 million people speak English as a second or third language.[2] For a refugee, knowing how to speak English in an English-speaking country brings work opportunities, understanding, and perhaps most valuable, some kind of acceptance from new neighbors and communities.

My old housemate Julia used to work as a caseworker for World Relief in Nashville. She was the first person to meet a refugee family at the airport and the first to take them to their new apartment in a complex just a few blocks off Nolensville Pike. She was the first one to take them to Kroger and show them how to find good deals to keep within their settlement budget. And she was the one who would show them what letters looked like and how they formed the words they would need.

But the thing is, whereas many of us clock out at 5:00 five evenings a week and don't think about work until the next morning, Julia carries the refugees with her everywhere. She carries them in her anecdotes, in her photographs, and in her prayers. They're not simply refugees or asylees for her; they're her family. They're the ones she wants to hang out with, eat with, and grow with.

When you work as a caseworker, you see a lot. You see the hope for work and peaceful life in parents' eyes. In the teenagers you see the nerves and anxiety about starting school in the middle of the semester. You see the administration that has to keep projects afloat and make the numbers work. You see the lists with new names and faces, joining a help program that's already tightly stretched.

There are several groups that help refugees and immigrants when they first arrive in Nashville. Catholic Charities and World Relief are only two of them, but between them both, they work to settle 1,000 cases a year. When you realize one case can be a family of ten, you start to see the number of lives being dealt with. For each case that caseworkers are given, they act as the bridge to American culture and life. Most of these families are starting from scratch and need the very basics. Caseworkers help them get their social security numbers, go for doctor checkups, enroll their children in school, learn how to use public transportation, read, speak, and write in English, and apply for jobs before their settlement funds run out.

Children of refugees are usually fairly fluent by the time they are ten years old because of school, but for the parents it's always more difficult. A lot of the adults may be illiterate in their own language or have a completely different script from the Latin alphabet we use, so although teachers may use worksheets or alphabets to give the basics, just being taught a new word can be the dearest and most needed achievement. Regardless of how long it takes someone to learn a new language, most refugee organizations will have an allotted amount of money for each case for only about six months. After that they must work, earn their own way, and survive.

Julia remembers a Bhutanese man who had been in the States for a while and had just gotten a job in the laundry rooms in one of Nashville's malls. He was living with his retired parents and had just gotten this job. Work and having a good work ethic are essential to Bhutanese people. On his first day he worked a twelve-hour shift in an extremely hot room without a break. When he finished his shift, he went home and hanged himself. He hadn't spoken to anyone. He already suffered from depression, both from his time in a refugee camp and because of a health condition that left him with very bad bumps all over his skin. But that he didn't have the language to communicate his fears and anxieties is a bitter reminder of language's power and the isolation of those around us.

New workplaces and schools are nearly always nerve-racking at first—being new, unknown, different, not knowing the social rituals and pecking order, just being the odd one out. For so many refugee families, adjusting to their new country brings the same worries as well as a few added ones. Not only are they expected to try to assimilate to American culture; they also need to learn the unwritten subtleties of the country. It's no wonder their caseworkers become their counselors, confidants, and defenders.

The Exodus Project in Indianapolis has a program to tackle these unspoken cultural rules. They teach how to fill in job application forms, how to report a problem to the apartment office, how to write checks, and what job interviews are like. They help them understand the cultural and linguistic parts of American life, from behavior habits and proper hygiene to employer expectations and verbal and non-verbal communications.

* * *

When I first met Kani, she was living in a small Section 8 apartment on the other side of Shelby Avenue, not far from where Julia and I lived. She was living alone with her three-year-old son, Guled, who was a bit of a firecracker and determined to find candy on me. She knew some English and told me her story, with Julia's help, of how she came from Somalia to Nashville.

She told me of her father leaving the family in Yemen, where they had run to escape the civil war. She told me of her mother dying in Ethiopia and of living with her uncle, who beat her to make her more submissive. She told me about the female circumcision (female genital mutilation) she endured without anaesthetic or clean instruments—a common practice in parts of Africa and Arabia. She told me of the planned arranged marriage to a man old enough to be her grandfather and how she ran to Mogadishu in the middle of the war to hide from her uncle. She met Guled's father and married, but her uncle wanted her back and used violence and fear to run her out of Somalia and into this new country.

When I last saw Kani, she was waiting for Guled's father to join them. She was nearing the end of the six-month settlement funding but still couldn't speak English very easily. In Somali culture it's taboo for women to leave their children with babysitters, so women lose out on education, work, and something of their own.

It's this clash of loyalties to the original country and the new home culture in refugees' lives that makes some people question their desire to be here and to make this their home. For a lot of us, it's simple. But maybe thinking new geography automatically creates home dilutes the ties of family, history, and identity that make us who we are. Maybe it's through time, friendships, relationships, and new experiences in this new geography that the shift happens.

In 2008, Julia began the Harbor Nashville to tell refugees she was prepared to put in the time with them. The Harbor functions just as its name suggests. It's a community of friends and small groups creating a place of refuge, protection, and safety for their new refugee friends in the time and resources they spend with them. Through this small organization Julia has been able to connect couples and individuals to the often hidden refugee communities of people who live close by them.

Christina and Ryan Rado help a Somali family of ten through The Harbor. They take them to the doctor, help with homework, and most urgent for the parents, they spend time patiently speaking in English. Diane Kilmer is a wonderful lady who has become like a sister to an Iraqi lady whose husband left her for a younger woman when she became ill with rheumatoid arthritis. Diane visited her when she was sick and helped her move into a new Section 8 home and find small jobs like cleaning.

Julia and her husband Jesse spend time with a Somali family of eight that I met at Christmas in 2008. We visited them with other friends and brought gifts that the Ibrahims had put on their Christmas wish list. They were things like school books, stationery, socks, shoes, and winter coats. Their youngest son was a typical five-year-old and ripped open his box before the rest. But the dad sat back in his seat looking over at all of us and kept saying, "This is the first time anyone has ever done this for us."

The efforts of The Harbor and other organizations like it aren't short-term fixes. They aren't Band-Aids over the issue of there being more refugees than caseworkers and charities.[3] This is adoption. Julia and the others take these families into their lives. There's a commitment involved that in all honesty has scared some people off. Unlike many organizations The Harbor Nashville doesn't require money as much as time, patience, and friendship. These three things are probably the hardest to give. They involve truly knowing a person beyond their name and place of birth. They demand vulnerability in both parties and a sacrifice by we who have been called to embrace.

Approximately 74,600 refugees entered the U.S.[4] in 2009. They live in major cities from California to Texas.[5] Of 74,600 refugees, I know two by name—Kani, who has since moved to Seattle, and Neineh, the young International studies graduate who now works with Exodus in Indianapolis, helping other Burmese people settle in.[6]

That I know the names of only two refugees speaks volumes about a divide between the foreigner and the local—a divide that grieves God to no end. In Deuteronomy we are told just how close these people are to God: "He defends the cause of the fatherless and the widow, and loves the alien, giving him food and clothing" (10:18). God does not just care or show a mild interest in the plight of those on the outside; he uses the word "love." God involves himself completely by clothing and feeding them. Jesus reiterates this sentiment when sitting on the Mount of Olives one day: "I was a stranger and you invited me in" (Matthew 25:35). And that is the bottom line. We've been invited to love like God, to allow strangers into our busy, relentless, safe lives. We've been invited to help make someone feel at home.

Rachel and Nate Graeser are living in LA. She has just applied for Teach for America, and he's in seminary. They're a long way from Chiang Rai in northern Thailand where they lived and worked during their first year of marriage. Rachel was in

New York when she first read about human trafficking and child sex prostitution in particular. What she read made her book a flight out to Thailand. She went with a motley group of friends and a trusty camera to collect firsthand stories from the people living through one of the world's most dark and sickening times. During that first trip, Rachel and her group met one girl in particular who deeply affected them. After months of interviewing children in the red light district, they met Cat in Bassan village, where the Sold Project mostly works now. Cat was nine years old at the time, in fourth grade, and had lost her mother to AIDS.

Being an orphan in Thailand has an immediate effect. There are no funds to finish school or to gain access to basics such as medicine, food, and clothing. Orphans are at the mercy of relatives or kindly neighbors who are already pressed looking after their own children. Being an orphan leaves a child desperate and vulnerable and the ideal target for those searching for child sex workers. For Rachel, then, it was a bitter miracle to meet Cat when she did. Although Cat had lost her mother, she hadn't been lost to the underworld yet. It was probably then that Rachel's trip became about preventing rather than just witnessing these hardships.

Most of the young women and children working in Thailand's sex trade are from the northern provinces, where they work in rice paddies on land they do not own and earn approximately $4.00 a day. The reality is that for some families, selling your child into prostitution may seem like the only lifeline you have. For the people in the Hill tribes in the Chiang Rai region, the injustices run deeper. The Thai government refuses to recognize this marginalized group as Thai citizens.[7] They are denied access to education, medical care, or even basic jobs and work.

Some of the Hill tribes' children attend local schools in Chiang Rai through the help of local volunteer groups that care for them during the semester and see them home for the holidays. But without the full support of their government, these children remain in a terrible place of having to use their one resource to bring their family some money.

In the last decade, Thailand's commercial sex industry has grown and added into the multi-billion dollar global industry, with hundreds of thousands of children, predominately girls, being exploited in the middle of it all.[8] Over the last twenty years, non-profit organizations have sprung up to fight this chilling practice, and scores have been rescued and rehabilitated. Yet, so many still cross the borders from neighboring Cambodia, Laos, and Burma to join those from the northern provinces—to sell their bodies.

It may be surprising then to know that if you were to get a moment to ask Thai children about their futures, you would hear them speak about dreams of becoming doctors, teachers, and owning their own businesses. It is for this very reason that The Sold Project decided to aim for the root of the problems and help prevent children falling into these traps by offering them an option and hope. They provide a holistic hope through a scholarship program, human trafficking awareness discussions, a mentorship program that partners children with a Thai college student, and a newly built resource center where they hang out with friends, get support for their high school exams, and are given the chance to simply play.

In much of the developing world, the first people to miss out on education are women and girls. Girls in the poorest 20 percent of households are far less likely to even attend school, let alone finish their primary education.[9] Since the MDG targets were set, there has been some slow improvement, reducing the gap between boys and girls in school in Southeastern Asia, with around ninety-six girls in school for every one hundred boys.[10] But by the time the children reach high school and college, the number of girls starts to dive again as they become wives and mothers.

In lots of countries, educating girls is seen as a waste of time and money as their future roles will mostly be filled with subsistence farming and raising children. This isn't housewifery as we know it. These young women will not have the broad options of what to feed their families each evening or the help of washing machines and dishwashers to get through the daily chores. Instead, their lives become intense and unrelenting labor. The simple necessity of water means they will spend untold hours every day collecting water and carrying it in jerry cans on their backs to their homes for washing, cooking, drinking, and cleaning. For many women and girls, this is life as they know it, but things have grown more difficult with more economic hardships, more unemployment, less infrastructure, and more men prepared to convince them into sex work.

* * *

I once watched a video of a Harvard professor speaking about justice.[11] He spoke about what it was, what it looked like and whom it was for. He asked, How much equality does a just society require? He asked whether it was fair for the wealthy to help the poor when they had worked hard to earn their own income. He spoke about morals and ethics, responsibility and the individual. He was talking in front of some of the brightest, most diligent, and most privileged young people in the States. He was asking them to imagine if things were different and they weren't in the position they were in, what would life be like for them? Would it be fair?

He talked to them about justice and noted education's role in giving everyone a fair start in life. With education, jobs start to open up, which means having the funds for housing, food, clothing, and medicine. With education, we get more than knowledge; we gain life skills—organization, perseverance, commitment, adaptability, resourcefulness, and creativity. We gain things, not just for our futures, but for this moment and all the challenges it brings.

When a Harvard professor, who is most likely doing very well financially (judging by the high college fees), admits that without equal access some of us will never get a chance to develop and create a decent life, we know something needs to be fixed.

* * *

At one point in time at Babel in Shinar we all spoke the same language. The word "babel" comes from the Hebrew *Bābhel*, translated from Akkadian and meaning "gate of god." We know the story of Babel—how people decided to build a spectacular ziggurat tower that the Mesopotamians were building everywhere. The Mesopotamians called the towers things like "the house of the link between heaven and earth" or "the house of the seven guides of heaven and earth." Our ancestors all wanted fame and commemoration and so lost their ability to understand each other and brought about the mass confusion we've been in ever since.

Since Babel, other languages have been shared all over the world with their empires, like Latin before the rise and replacement of English. Except this time we aren't trying to build towers, but economies and industries. But perhaps there's another language that existed and continues to be shared among us—the one of human need. The need to be healthy, fed, safe, clean, sheltered, loved, and happy.

Regardless of where we were scattered or what dialect or tongue we speak, our needs remain the same. It was George Washington Carver who said, "Education is the key to unlock the golden door of freedom," and its truth becomes even deeper when we see it played out in the lives of refugees and asylees. To them, learning isn't a chore or a test of endurance to last until Friday afternoon. It isn't to be despised or relegated as "boring." It's a road that leads to somewhere bright.

I've never placed education and survival in the same thought, but that is what it has meant to so many refugees and children who would otherwise have become mere statistics. Having the language to ask questions or give information means refugees in the States can speak to their coworkers and be more than life-size images of their war-torn countries of origin. Having a full and complete education means a vulnerable child has options, openings to future job training, employment, and a free life.

But this isn't something we can expect governments to fix with time and limited funding programs. God tells us, "When an alien lives with you in your land, do not mistreat him. The alien living with you must be treated as one of your native-born. Love him as yourself" (Leviticus 19:33-34). It's us he's talking to. It's us he's waiting for. And of course Jesus himself lived out those commands in his open communication with the Roman centurion, the Syro-Phoenician woman, and in his renowned message of the Good Samaritan.

So maybe our main preoccupation shouldn't be whether these people should be in our country, our neighborhood, or why they are here, but to know them, to know their stories, to get involved, and to draw them inside our community. There's something wonderful in knowing there is a way to navigate through the darkness that surrounds. Our mandate is pure and direct: to see people, to love them, and to do what we can to help them thrive.

Knock, knock

Ever considered hosting a foreign exchange student?

It's quite easy to set up, and you can pick the countries you want the students to be from.

It's a great thing to do if you want to learn another language or brush up on a bit of Spanish, German, or maybe some Turkish.

It's also a unique opportunity to get to know people from different cultures.

You can find more information at:
http://www.ayusa.org
http://www.asse.com

Watch the documentary *Sold*

Better yet, show *Sold* as part of a Sunday School class, small group meeting, or quilting circle (Do people still do that? If not they definitely should! Who doesn't love quilts?)

After that pass a hat and send some money their way. They're wonderful people who are providing education to children in Thailand who are at risk of being trafficked.

To buy the documentary, go to:
http://shop.thesoldproject.com/products/the-sold-project-thailand-dvd

On the road

Not sure if you know how your city's bus system runs? Or maybe even where the bus stops are? Now is your chance to find out.

Why not take a refugee out on the town as a welcome/orientation Saturday afternoon?

You never know; you might actually like having someone else do all the driving. Oh yes, and don't forget you can take your bike along for the ride too!

Be a patron of the letters

School can be fun. It can also be a refuge and the path out of poverty.

Did you know in medieval times, monks used to give lessons at the monasteries to boys who wanted to become priests or who wanted to do something outside the cloister?

Remember the least likely ones to get through school are girls and orphans. For $1 a day you could help make them scribes.

Find out more at:
http://www.planusa.org/waystogive
https://thesoldproject.com/donate/

Picnic exchange

The sun is out, the sky is blue, the grass is ready; it just needs you. Cheesy, yes, but honestly, when the weather is so beautiful, it must be a sin to be cooped up indoors.

What are some of your favorite places on a sunny day? Your city's big green park, you say? The one perfect for picnics?

How about preparing a few dishes, inviting a refugee family to prepare one or two of their favorite dishes, and having a food swap in the park?

It's cheap, cheerful, and neighborly. And you may just expand your palate a bit!

Book sale!

Except it's not one, really. It's more like a giveaway.

How many of your old school books do you still have in your parents' garage? Probably plenty—they're in those boxes that are covered in cobwebs.

Don't let them grow any more mold. Organizations all over the world are teaching children and adults how to speak, read, write, and listen in English, and they're always in need of materials and resources, whether used or new.

Check out the Sold Project's big book drive and help keep a child out of trafficking and into hope.

Go to: http://www.treeoflifebooks.com/soldproject to find out more about how to send your books at no cost to you.

Lexis

Vocabulary is the color of language.

Write down a list of twenty random words and phrases. For the next twenty-four hours the words and phrases on this list will be your entire language bank. Yes, even when you need to talk to a member of the public. (Choose your experiment day wisely.)

When you've finished, you'll have a bit of an idea of what it feels like not to be able to communicate.

Feeling brave? Check out the refugee settlement offices near you and see how you can volunteer some time to teach English.

8
SEX, SLAVES, *and* SALES

"I pray because
I believe in
love."

—EDITH PIAF[1]

The Super Bowl is the crown of the great American football game. When you say "Super Bowl," funny commercials, the halftime show, the national anthem, hot dogs, nachos, astronomical ticket prices, and team pride come to mind. Human trafficking does not. Yet human trafficking was one of the biggest earners at this year's Super Bowl in Dallas, Texas. Every year, 100,000 American teens and trafficked women are exploited in the sex trade and used in sex rings around the stadium to feed the demand of thousands of men.[2] This is a number that should disturb and offend. It should cause us to lament the state of things; it should cause us to react.

For a lot of us, human trafficking has become synonymous with Southeast Asia. If we've heard the term, then usually images of Thailand and campaigns like Call and Response[3] are our first thoughts, and justly so, as Asia has become a breeding ground for an industry that is spinning a net profit of $32 billion a year.[4] Around 600,000 to 800,000 men, women, and children are forced across international borders every year for two purposes—forced labor or the sex trade. Nearly two million children are being hemmed into the commercial sex trade.

If you are sold as a sex slave, regardless of your gender or age, you can be expected to "service" at least ten clients a day. If you are in a country in Southeast Asia, the going rate for you will be $30.[5] If you fight back you will be beaten until you can't remember how it started. You may be raped by your owners, you may watch a friend die, you may be deprived of food and water.

You will be kept in brothels so closely guarded your sense of time in the outside world will wane. There will be no end unless the brothel is raided, death comes for you, or you gather the courage to run away.

Human trafficking is one of the hardest topics in the social justice field. It is brutal and unforgiving. It doesn't care for our sensibilities or comfort, and the worst part is it is not merely the subject of Hollywood films like *Taken*—it is a nightmare reality that earns as much as the illegal arms trade.[6] Slavery is not dead, despite the great efforts of Abraham Lincoln, William Wilberforce, and others who have come after them. With around twenty-seven million people trapped in the world's third biggest criminal activity, modern slavery is alive and thriving. People are still bought against their will and forced into an existence that denies them dignity, rights, or any safety. People are still seen as commodities without will or power, to use and reuse until there is nothing left.

Somaly Mam was sold into slavery as a child by a man who posed as her grandfather. Like the Hill Tribe people of northern Thailand, she's from a minority group from the Mondulkiri province in Cambodia. And like the Hill Tribe her community is plagued with poverty, lack of access to the basics, very little education, and a narrow future. Somaly worked in a brothel with several other children and endured torture and rape. She was told she would survive if she kept her silence. But when she watched her friend be viciously murdered, she ran out of fear that she would meet the same fate.

Life in a brothel isn't life. The descriptions, facts, and stories about it sound closer to an abyss. Children as young as three years old can be sold by their parents or siblings for money.

They're bought because they're virgins and it's thought virgins can heal AIDS, make their clients live longer, or make their clients remain young. So high is the demand for virgins, girls are stitched and re-stitched to be re-sold as virgins.

The traffickers use hate-filled fear to force these women and children to stay. They are beaten brutally and punished if they disobey. One girl describes how she was put in "the cage" for refusing to take between ten and fifteen clients a day. She was a child and was physically very small at the time. Her captors put her in the cage without food or water, beat her, urinated on her, and then gave her electrical shocks to make her submit.[7]

The depths of this human tragedy become clearer with every woman who gives her story. One former trafficked victim tells of the first client she had. When he finished he literally threw her aside across the room and into a corner. She remembers bleeding heavily and trying to crawl back to the bed, but feeling like she was going crazy. She remembers feeling that she had lost all sense of being a person.[8]

In many ways Cambodia is as hurt as its people. Pol Pot's genocide in the 1970s took a lot of the wealthy and educated as well as any structure. Cambodia was left in poverty and with a meager education and one third of the population earning less than $360 a year. Brothel owners can make that same amount in one month from just four sex workers, so they bribe police and government officials to turn a blind eye.

It's because of all of this that Somaly Mam started handing out condoms to brothel workers and taking the sick ones to clinics. She now has three centers in Cambodia sheltering and rehabilitating 150 women and children. Her teams have reached at least 5,000 women in Phnom Phen, and they continue to work because human trafficking does not slow down.

* * *

AnnaLynne McCord is a justice fighter first and a Hollywood actress second. Speaking out against human trafficking has become her most earnest fight. I spoke to AnnaLynne on her break between shooting scenes for an episode of the TV series *90210*. She speaks quickly and so passionately that you can't help but start to see how desperate this situation is. This isn't zeal from a growing trend, but from someone who has shared and seen the very real pain of six-year-olds recovering from being sex slaves.

She talks about her last visit to Phnom Phen with her older sister and best friend last Christmas and New Year. She talks about the school supplies and computers they brought over after convincing her agency and the *90210* cast and crew to donate resources. And she talks plenty about Somaly Mam. Somaly Mam is AnnaLynne's hero. It's funny hearing an actress and a Noble Humanitarian award winner sound so awestruck, but she is. She's in awe of Somaly's courage and commitment and her fixation on building a sustainable future for these girls and women rather than raging at the past.

At first I find it odd. The worlds of Hollywood and human trafficking seem leagues apart. One celebrates beauty, media obsession, and being captured by cameras, while the other is an ugly, secretive trade that has hidden people in the dark. But perhaps their partnership speaks more about the collaboration that must happen in order to reach those who still need to hear the message of what's happening to our neighbors across the globe. Celebrities are beloved and popular. If they share an awareness message on Twitter their followers will Google it before they've reached the end of the sentence. If they give an interview and mention a statistic or some work that's being done, chances are someone will follow up. They'll follow links and read more around the topic. They'll scour photos and watch films related to it. Maybe they'll even open up a bit more to the subject because someone they respect is fighting for it.

AnnaLynne starred in the film *Amexica*, which follows the path of a pair of con artists who "rent" a Mexican boy to sell and use at their whim. It's a short film, but its heart is loud, even more so because of the little boy who cannot speak English and cannot communicate or understand what's happening to him. The film reminds us again of just how cruel humans can be in their sins—in stealing another's voice and words. In stealing their life and their breath, which is a holy, sacred breath.

AnnaLynne acts because of the edge it brings. She acts for the little rescued four-year-old girl she held in Cambodia and the ones she doesn't know. She acts because it leads to advocacy and campaigns, signed petitions, and hopefully passed laws. Delving into the world of human trafficking is a dark place. It's dark in its content and it's dark to your soul. It's a topic that can pull you under its load and cause you to lose all hope in humanity. But it's an age-old truth that says without hope, we're lost. And so I believe AnnaLynne when she says it's only by us coming together and uniting as a whole that this thing will end.

* * *

Atlanta is a bustling city. We know that it's famous for its music scene (John Mayer's humble beginnings), for being the spiritual heart of the Civil Rights Movement and the home to nearly 4.9 million people in the metropolitan area.[9] What's less known are some of the more sobering and chilling facts about the city, collected and shared in a short film by girls no older than fifteen years old.

Every month, around 500 underage girls are trafficked into Atlanta to supply the demands of 7,200 men who come to the city for sex. Fourteen years old is the average age of these girls, though they've been known to be as young as nine. A further one hundred to 150 girls are raped for profit each weekend.[10] The phrase "raped for profit," also used by International Justice Mission (IJM), is as severe as it is true. This is not just prostitution, but children being held prisoner for an average of seven years before they die or are killed.[11]

Perhaps it is even more distressing to learn that Atlanta's Hartsfield-Jackson International Airport has become the trading floor where traffickers meet clients, take them to child sex slaves, and then return them to catch their flights home to join their own families.[12] The idea that men will leave their families to have paid sex with children brings human trafficking home in a way not much else can. It isn't just that these are children being violated, but the fact that it's everyday individuals who are visiting them. These children are not seen as people with names, birthdays and favorite colors, but as objects to satisfy an appetite.

There is a scene toward the end of the movie *A Time to Kill* in which the lawyer is giving his final speech to the Mississippi jury about the rape of a small ten-year-old African-American girl. He retells the girl's story by setting the scene of that afternoon. He uses words and imagery to pull the jury in, and he's very passionate about it, but then he closes by saying, "now imagine she was white."[13] We could subsitute the word "white" with any number of words that make the story more applicable for our own lives, but the point of this story is that it jolts and electrifies the jurors and all of us watching because it tears us open and exposes how deeply detached from problems we are until they become personal.

I'm curious as to if that was what Jesus was getting at when he said, "Whatever you did for one of the least of these brothers of mine, you did for me" (Matthew 25:40). Perhaps until we see others as ourselves or as Jesus himself, we won't see a lasting end to these horrible practices.

* * *

Jodi De Souza has been a friend for years; she's been the artistic director of The Humble Theatre Company for four years. In all that time she has never shied away from controversy or bringing it into our lives. Her work isn't just for entertainment or art, but for speaking to us about things from which we'd much rather run.

A couple of summers ago she and a small group of actors devised a play called *No Sale*, about London's sex industry. They held it at a small pub venue with the bed in the center of the floor so that we were right inside the brothel and there was nowhere else to look. The play followed one girl's journey from Eastern Europe to London for work, only to find herself stuck paying a debt to the traffickers by serving as many clients as they would send to her. I remember a few people walking out in the middle of performance; I thought they probably left because the content was so brutish and loud and intense, but later I found out they left because the characters swore.

Sometimes we read the Bible and we see its rules and laws. We see its commands and limitations, things set up to be a safety rail as we clamber through this life. But sometimes we read these strict orders and become fixed on them. The answer to every situation is there in black and white, and when fellow pilgrims discourage us from using bad language, we hold it like a standard flag to mark that we're obedient and living the Bible and living with God. And somehow we miss what's truly important—love, sacrifice, life.

When John the Baptist sees the Pharisees and Sadducees approaching he launches in and calls them a "brood of vipers" (Matthew 3:7). He's mad at them because they've separated themselves from the people they were supposed to love and serve and are completely oblivious to it. They've set high, legalistic standards while maintaining their own political and economic interests. They've deemed everybody lower than themselves. And yet even though we read this and know this, we still can separate ourselves from someone's blatant need because it offends and good people don't use that kind of language.

Those audience members were able to leave; all of us were free to. At any moment we could all simply stand, take our coats and bags, and leave what we found unpleasant and what made us uncomfortable. The fact that these women and children in brothels and holes up and down our countries cannot do so only magnifies the severe prison sex slaves are in. Sex trafficking rattles us. It astounds us because it has grown so big and powerful and so far-reaching. Sex trafficking offends because it takes what should be pure and good and distorts it. But it still needs us to face it head on and acknowledge its reality in all its ugliness. It needs to outrage us into making a stand.

One of the biggest criticisms we all tend to hear is, Where is God while all this is happening? Where is God when the traffickers gouge out the Cambodian woman's eye to teach her a lesson? Where is God when a child contracts HIV after he's been raped? Where is God when a woman's husband takes her to a room and sells her to torturers for $300?

There's in account in the middle of 2 Samuel (chapter 13) that centers on David and his family. David is an older king now, and his children from different wives have grown up too. But family ties in Jewish custom are supposed to be strong, so it shouldn't matter that they have different mothers. But then we read that Amnon lures his half sister, Tamar, to his bedside by pretending to be sick. She's a good Jewish girl, so she goes and bakes bread and brings it to him. But when she comes, he sends the servants away and rapes her calling it love.

The story afterward sounds so similar to the ones of sex workers it's disquieting. Amnon starts to hate her with an intense hatred and she is left to pile ashes on her head and live with her brother Absalom as a disgraced woman. And David's response to this? He was furious, and yet he didn't do anything about Amnon and lost his family to revenge and war afterward.

God's involvement is not mentioned, but that doesn't mean he wasn't there. That doesn't mean he wasn't grieved by what happened to Tamar or by David's inaction. That this story was recorded at all shows something of his heart about injustice. It's not swept away and ignored because it deals with taboo subjects like incest and rape. It's not hidden away because it shows a weak father and a failing family. God deals with the difficult and wicked parts of life; he listens and really hears the cry and tears of those hurt, and he wants us to do the same.

Human trafficking has become such a mammoth crime, it's an empire all of its own. So many are involved, from brothel owners to kidnappers, from bribed police officers and judges to those who demand this kind of sex. Human trafficking works and grows because there is a demand. Traffickers will continue to buy and steal people; others will pawn their children, wives and sisters to supply that demand. If it's really to end, perhaps we need to go to the root first.

From research findings as well as documentary hidden cameras, men have been found to be the buyers and consumers of sex trafficking victims. Their identities, occupations, and addresses are mostly unknown. They are faceless individuals that for a myriad of reasons choose to pay to abuse. A report from the Office to Monitor and Combat Trafficking in persons (TIP Office) tells us that despite common belief, the majority are not lonely, sexually unfulfilled men. Many have several sexual partners and a lot are satisfied with their wives and partners. But they all want sex acts their wives and partners will not do. They want the thrill of buying another person and being free to humiliate, degrade, and hurt another person without consideration.[14] Many have said the experience is not rewarding, but they return repeatedly to use fear, power, and control over the sex workers.

But these buyers are only part of the demand. Their money certainly makes the machines of exploitation work, but to say it is all irrefutably their fault is to oversimplify. We live in a culture that indirectly approves of the sex industry despite its controversies. We have different names for it too, like strip clubs and escort and outcall agencies. But their objectives are still the same—using women for sexually-driven entertainment for willing consumers.

Nashville is notorious for its strip clubs and its ever-growing porn industry. That women have become objects on film, on a stage, through a peephole or on the Internet is simply accepted as freedom. Freedom for the woman who is regarded as liberated, empowered, and independent—despite being at the mercy of the men who will pay to watch.

Without realizing it we have become desensitized to what is happening to us and how we see each other. We accept when a group of twentysomethings prance and dance around in music videos acting out the very things that are demanded of trafficked victims in brothels. Somehow we've separated their experiences from our excesses. And governments are strangely confusing about this. On one hand human trafficking is condemned for breaching human rights while the other hand tries to legalize prostitution and so perpetuates the markets where these victims will be sent.

In 2002, Germany legalized prostitution to offer women health benefits, retirement plans, a chance to sign up with trade unions, and the chance to pay taxes. With buyers free from prosecution, the demand shot up, and so did the number of trafficked women who were the least likely and least able to use the government's promised benefits. Those trafficked into Germany went up 70 percent since 2005, including children.

But when governments and policy makers work to protect the human lives involved, there's a shift in our culture and our way of thinking. Sweden, the birthplace of Ikea, Saab, and the Nobel Prize for Peace, showed how things could be changed. In 1999, they made it illegal to buy sex, but left it legal to sell it. The results were quick. Men were deterred from buying, and the trafficker didn't buy as many slaves. In five years the number of those trafficked into Sweden went down 40 percent, and in 2008 there were 400 human trafficking cases compared to 17,000 in neighboring Norway.

In the U.S. too, local governments have worked to cut the demand down—like Atlanta mayor Shirley Franklin's Dear John Campaign, which used videos and posters to make clear: "Not in my city."[15] And even during the Dallas Super Bowl, massive efforts were made to curb the trafficking. The city put billboard posters up with the message "Not for me" while Dallas Cowboy Jay Ratliff filmed a video message for the thousands who would be attending the game: "Real men don't buy children. They don't buy sex."[16]

Throughout the U.S. the growing collaboration between local law enforcement, government, and neighborhood groups shows the steadily turning tide. In Kansas City, 250 neighbors joined together with Steve Wagner from Renewal Forum to put their new role as the U.S.'s first anti-sex trafficking model city into practice. Around 1,650 minors are being exploited in the Kansas City metropolitan area, with another 4,300 in Missouri and 2,300 in Kansas. The community members decided they had had enough of such figures and wanted to create an environment that made it impossible for the trade to continue.[17]

Neighbors are learning how to spot when someone is trapped, how to rescue a victim, how restoration happens, how they can reduce the demand, and what local government's action should be. They are finding out more about the nature and extent of the problem in their area. Perhaps therein lies our answer; this isn't something just for activists and campaigners, nor is it a horrible problem happening in a faraway poor land. It is happening here in our neighborhoods, cities, and towns: around 300,000 children and teens are trafficked in the U.S.[18]

We all need to be involved. We all need to be affected for a lasting change to happen. When we can mourn and lament the things that happen, maybe it will pull us into one place of seeing these people not as "others" but as ourselves. When we can grieve our sins in ashes, perhaps then we'll understand God isn't at a lofty distance, ignoring these crimes, but is filled with love that burns so brightly it's washing out the darkness.

Amos' prophecies to Israel read like an ode to social justice. His every word is earnest, almost feverish. He holds a magnifying glass to Israel, and he does the same to us. God wasn't interested in word-perfect rituals and offerings that didn't have a devoted heart behind them. Amos goes into the heart of us when he says, "Therefore the prudent man keeps quiet in such times, for the times are evil" (Amos 5:13). How many of us feel we're no match for these crimes that link countries, governments, the collective, and the individual? And yet without us those trapped and literally held behind barbed wire fences have no escape, no emancipation, which goes against everything we are.

When Jesus read from the Torah in Nazareth, after surviving the desert, he laid his purpose out for us. He came with good news for the poor because they were known to him. He came to be the defender of the oppressed, imprisoned, and for those who couldn't see any of the troubles that were right around them (see Luke 4:17-18). His heart hasn't changed; he's simply asking if we'll continue along with him.

Read the missing posters

How many of us have actually stopped to check out the missing children posters at our local post office or grocery store? Most of the American teens in the sex industry are runaways. Finding them is the first step to getting them help and keeping them out of brothels.

Stay on the lookout with North American Missing Persons Network at http://www.nampn.org

Become an abolitionist

Trafficked women don't get to leave their brothel. The system is such that there is no way out and there is no freedom.

They must be rescued. Thus, it is up to you and me to say something if we see something suspicious.

Raid and rescue is the only way out.

If you see something that looks like trafficking, call the Trafficking Hotline: 1-888-3737-888.

For more information, go to: http://www.polarisproject.org/

Big brother's watching

Try Kansas City's example of banding the neighborhood together. There's power in numbers and in community.

How about introducing it by screening a human trafficking documentary at a church or community hall, and maybe asking if the local police would send a representative for Q & A time.

For further group training on what to look out for and recognize, check out http://www.exoduscry.com/

Oh, and invite a teen to come along as well.

Root deep

Human trafficking feeds off its buyers.

Millions are trapped in the illegal sex trade because someone is willing to pay for them.

Be on your guard. Sign up with:
http://x3watch.com
http://www.internetsafety.com

Running costs

A lot of the women and children who finally manage to get out of sex trafficking do so because someone staked the place out, sent in rescue teams, and broke them out.

Escape in that closely guarded world is near impossible. A lucky few will literally run away.

But rescue is just the start of their new lives.

Most of the organizations that work to rehabilitate and restore these women and children can do so only with your help.

You can:
1. Go to the website of your choice and see how you can donate.
2. Get creative—and in shape—and do a sponsored run and run them out of brothels with the money you raise.

Amexica

America and Mexico have had their issues: the Mexican-American war, illegal immigration, drugs, and gangs. But now something else is on the scene.

Get some friends together and some popcorn and watch the short film *Amexica*. It tells the human trafficking story in a different light and puts the lens on what's happening here in our backyard.

9
GARDENERS
and
GREENHOUSES

Our mandate
in the garden
was clear: work
the earth and
take care of it.
It wasn't just
for Adam.

We were gardeners once. Our garden was perfect, with plants, trees, rivers, and seas that had just been made. We had animals that we understood and named. We had fruits and vegetables aplenty to eat. We had a paradise to fashion and build in, to add to and love. We had our Eden.

When God decided to make Adam, it was for love, to reflect his image and to give the earth a guardian. After he molded him out of clay, he blessed him and said, "Be fruitful and increase in number; fill the earth and subdue it" (Genesis 1:28). It was never about control and domination, but representation. We were made in God's image to be his representatives and to protect and develop the earth with the kindness and respect of its creator. We were stewards to his realm, here to care for nature and its animals. We were meant to prevent exploitation, waste, and ruin.

The environment as a social justice issue is an afterthought for most of us. Social justice is about people and fairness; the environment is seen as something about trees and pollution—things that don't have a soul. Environmentalists and Christians are at odds. The disputes are wide and entrenched; they go to the root of what we believe and where our loyalties lie and what we can trust.

Global warming is the biggest divider: is it real? How can we be sure? And where's the proof that it's humanity's fault? I remember when I first heard one of my roommates announce that global warming was all a tactic of some partisans and it wasn't real at all. For as long as I can remember going to school, I'd heard about this huge glass house that covered the entire world and was making it heat up like an oven that would melt the ice caps and then us next.

It was never an opinion or a probability; it was a fact. The earth was getting hotter because of carbon dioxide. It was because of our cars and towering chimney factories that chugged dirty smoke into the atmosphere. It was because we kept burning coal that was a fossil fuel from dinosaur bones and that was going to run out soon too. And it was because of old refrigerators that gave off a horrible CFC stench when they broke down. These things were all certain because of science and all of its repeated tests. But there are other thoughts now that make things less certain and raise questions about our role in all of it.

The earth has gotten warmer; scientists agree on that. The climate temperature has risen 0.8 degrees Celsius in the last one hundred years.[1] But this is where their agreements end. For some, the earth's temperature has always fluctuated and its plants and animals are perfectly able to adapt to meet the change. The earth is more resistant than we realize, and it's unlikely we'll see anything catastrophic from it. The seasons may be becoming longer, there may be stronger weather and changes in precipitation, but they doubt climate change will affect much at all in the long run.

When the tsunami hit on December 26, 2004, we were left flabbergasted. It killed around 230,000 people and ravaged Indonesia, Sri Lanka, India, and Thailand. The earth can be so silent and docile we barely notice it, but when tidal waves the size of ten-story buildings crash on coasts and kill whole families, we notice something very unsettling. Geologists who studied the natural disaster have seen that climate change affects not only the air and oceans but the earth's surfaces as well. When ice melts, the earth's crust rises back up in ways that cause earthquakes and bring on landslides and tsunamis.[2]

I remember when the earthquake shattered Haiti, I was in South Korea teaching English. It didn't affect me much at first because quakes and mudslides seemed to be happening all the time. But when we found out one of our fellow teachers couldn't reach his family in Haiti, it stopped being a global phenomenon and became small and personal and far too close to the bone. Haiti lost around 300,000 people in the earthquake, and thousands of homes and businesses were destroyed.

It's been over a year, but the images of rubble in streets, lost children, mourning locals, and utter confusion remain. The country is still forced to rely on grants to rebuild the capital, much of which was surrounded by slum cities, where most of the civilians died. More than one million people still live in tent cities in Port-au-Prince, like the one in Champs de Mars, where up to thirty people may share one tent.[3] Others have made their home along medians in roads.

Hurricane Katrina saw thousands of people lose lives and homes. The hurricane that hit them could not have been controlled by anyone, but the response to it could have been different—from the confused official planning that saw National Guard troops stuck waiting for a chain of command to be established[4] to the thousands of people trapped in the Superdome and the New Orleans Convention Center waiting for the storm to pass over before they would be given ice or water.[5] From the 350 miles of levees and flood walls that failed and saw the

Ninth Ward disappear to the U.S. Army Corps of Engineering that insisted it wasn't their fault until investigations showed poor designs and weak soil had been ignored.

And so we're left asking who's responsible for this climate change, and we find ourselves divided again. Some will call these tragedies acts of God—events caused without any human interference. When they are acts of God, we're excused and we're released. We're not to blame. Calling something an act of God calls nature rebellious and us innocent, but when we look over what is contributing to climate change and adding to natural disasters, it seems we aren't so innocent after all.

It is our gas guzzling cars that churn out methane gases and twenty pounds of carbon dioxide per gallon.[6] It is our incinerators and factories that chug out coal, gas, and oil every day. It is the deforestation to make room for farming that has lost us so many trees—trees that had kept the balance between carbon dioxide and oxygen for generations. It is us and our desire to have fast, mass-produced products like fast food that have led to the creation of industrial sized farms. Animals and corn are now grown to such an extent we have too much of them and too high a level of methane and nitrous oxide. Our insatiable desire to have resources on tap has meant a constant stream of burning fossil fuels and accelerated changes in the environment.

There are others who think differently though. Some scientists believe that 70 percent of the climate change happened before 1940 and the industrial oil drilling explosion of the 1970s[7] had nothing to do with it. There are some who would say all scientific research is merely probabilities and can't be used as certainties and so we definitely cannot be sure it's our fault. And even if it is our fault, there's nothing we can do about it now.

But we are the stewards. We're the ones called to take responsibility and to manage the world's resources properly. The psalmist described the earth as the Lord's and everything in it, and he made us the caretakers. Our mandate in the garden was clear: work the earth and take care of it. It wasn't just for Adam. Like the rest of the Bible, its message was for all who would come after. The world was never meant to be just a temporary place, an in-between stop. When God made it, he made it to last and formed it in celebration. He designed it for animals and man to live alongside each other with everything they would need. He made it for man to govern, but for he himself to still be there as a close and tangible presence (see Genesis 3:8). He created it so that every human could know there was a creator.

But then we were sent into exile. When we left we didn't only lose paradise; we went under a curse. And it wasn't just us who suffered; the land was cursed too. Isaiah says it clearly when he tells Israel: "Therefore a curse consumes the earth; its people must bear their guilt" (Isaiah 24:6). Isaiah is talking to Israel to shake them out of apathy. They are living apart from God and forgetting to be just and merciful, so they are judged. He tells them the earth will dry up and wither and be plundered and destroyed. The earth was to be punished because people had broken their peace with God. Isaiah's words are strong and uncomfortable; they feel out of place in our age of studied politics and reasoning. We have learned to argue, and we have learned to debate. We have learned to tell ourselves the environment is important, but it's not a matter of life or death.

There is a farmer in southwest Bangladesh named Mostafa who gave a speech to his small village. He spoke about the unbearably hot weather and the rains, which hadn't shown up and so had ruined his vegetable crops. A month later, cyclone Aila hit his area and he lost his home, farm, and the village where he gave his speech. His village had flood barriers because they were so close to the river, but they didn't have a backup plan for their agricultural economy.[8]

For years, scientists have been expecting the weather to worsen, but none thought they would see this much of it in our generation. Changes in our environment do have an effect, and for the most vulnerable, the effects are dramatic and absolute. As rainfall and temperature levels continue to change, so do people's livelihoods. In the 1960s pest-resistant seeds were engineered to grow farmers abundant harvests. They were heavily sold to developing countries, but the seeds needed stable conditions. Today's conditions are not only unsteady; they're unpredictable. And so with sudden changes in climate, crop yields have started to shrink and water has become more rare. With less food being produced, the price of grain naturally skyrockets, and people, especially the urban poor, who cannot grow their own food, are left in abject hunger.

But it doesn't stop there. As steady farming becomes less dependable, farmers are driven into the cities to look for work. The poor come in crowds and move into badly built shantytowns, which are more likely to be swept away in severe weather. They are more likely to have little to no sanitation in these slums, which only gets worse as water becomes scarce. They are more susceptible to diseases like malaria and diarrhea, especially due to their lack of health care to fight them.

Some say pushing the environment agenda is the equivalent of the social gospel, spreading the message of New Age pantheism by agreeing that our earth might be off balance. They say it puts too much stock in the creation rather than the creator. Some say this whole topic of the environment is an inflated piece of propaganda to scare and pressure us to change our lives and lose our comforts, like our several cars per family.

Others have said we need to cut emissions per head or per country. So we drive at slower speeds in certain zones and we pay a little extra on our plane tickets to cut carbon emissions. Still others say the governments and leaders need to change laws and bring in reforms to stop the damage that's being done, but it costs a lot to restructure whole industries. Many feel it also tampers with individual freedoms by regulating what companies or we ourselves are allowed to do.

Both of these arguments boil the issue of the environment down to choosing a side, being in one camp or the other. Both are adamant in their scientific findings and opinions and in the agendas they are trying to push. But our earth goes beyond who is right or wrong, who's honest or who's delusional; it's about what we do and have been called to do.

Right now, we produce mammoth amounts of waste every year. We throw away a lot. We toss out paper, cartons, tissue boxes, metal, clothes, shoes, plastic, and food. We create more than 250 million metric tons of waste every year that we store in landfills across the country.[9] We rarely if ever think about what happens to the garbage once the trucks come to empty the trash. We don't know about the sealed landfills that cannot be used again because they've been filled to capacity, or "leachate," the liquid that comes from the decomposing objects that can sometimes seep into the soil and into our waterways and contaminate freshwater supplies. Nor do we consider the aluminium can that we don't recycle that will sit unchanged in landfills for the next 500 years.

And it's not just our creeping level of trash that is an issue. We have consumed more resources in the last fifty years than ever before in history.[10] Our appetite for more has grown, and so have our industries. Just looking at how we eat shows as much. The *Food, Inc.* documentary that came out in 2008 put a microscope on our habits and our eating. Farming used to be something farmers did with tractors, farmhands, and barns. There were animals out to pasture and crops growing high. Back then there was a limit to how much they could grow and also how much we could consume. A farmer used to be able to grow twenty bushels of corn per acre and be grateful for the harvest.[11]

But then a food revolution of sorts happened. Suddenly we wanted fast food, and we wanted it all the time. Meals were no longer spent with the family; they were now to be short, speedy experiences to meet our increasingly busy lives. And with our new appetite we lost traditional farming with its love of the land in the process.

Suddenly we were clearing masses of land to build more farms that could hold more animals that could produce more products. The deforestation of Latin America spells out how big the problem became. Although forests cover 30 percent of the world's landmass, geographers believe in one hundred years all of our rainforests will have disappeared.[12] The land is cleared either for agriculture or urbanization, but mostly the former. Farmers want more land to grow crops like soy or for their livestock to graze on.[13] Rich countries go to Panama or Brazil and are granted logging rights with high concessions to log for tropical timber that is turned into furniture and flooring.[14]

That's not to say local farmers aren't adding to the problem of deforestation too. In Quiandeua, Brazil, "homesteader" policies give small farmers the right to slash and burn the forests wherever they want to. Farmers cut the trees at random to plant cassava, but the soil they are trying to farm has barely any nutrients in it. Usually within two years the farmers have given up and moved on, leaving the dead trees behind them.

And yet we still want more, so we plant and grow excesses of corn through government-sponsored programs that enable us to flood our corn on foreign markets in the developing world and to sell to the big food manufacturers on home turf. Corn has become the new staple. It's cheap to grow, due to the government's subsidization, and has more uses than just animal feed. It may be surprising to learn in just how many products corn can be found—from xanthan gum, which is found in salad dressings and mayonnaise, to sorbitol, which is usually found in candies and is used as a sugar substitute for diabetics.[15] But finding out the reasons why farmers and owners of Concentrated Animal Feeding Operation (CAFO) farms were feeding their cattle, swine, poultry, and even harvested salmon corn was even more troubling.

Corn helps animals bulk up, making them weigh-in ready for the factory in a fraction of the amount of time they would normally take on an ordinary and balanced diet. Considering we bought more than $110 billion worth of fast food and sodas in 2001,[16] it's in the industry's interest to meet the demand as quickly as they can. This leaves America's health to deteriorate while the manufacturers make huge profits.

Cows are built to eat grass in fields, but now they're eating grain in troughs, through narrow bars, pressed up tightly against each other. Subsidized corn, mass feeding farms, cleared forests, animals in cramped and inhumane conditions—all this is happening even though we were the ones who were called to be protectors. Scientists and engineers have been designing ways to use ethanol, another corn product, as a fuel instead of gas or diesel, but the cost on the land and animals hasn't gone unnoticed.

When E. coli O157:H7 started to be found in ground beef from corn-eating cattle, scientists soon noticed a pattern. There have been scores of cases of E. coli outbreaks; a recent one affected people in Maine and New York who ate beef from a Cargill plant in Minneapolis.[17] All these things make us see how far away we've come from God's idea of working the land and tending to the animals with love and respect.

At Sinai, after the Israelites had just been freed from slavery, God gave his people advice on how to sow and harvest their fields for six years and then allow them to lie fallow for a year. It was a custom that continued on, even through feudal times in Europe. But it wasn't just so the land could rest, but so we could rest as well. In that seventh, Sabbath year, Israel was supposed to allow the poor to use and eat whatever they found on the land; after they had finished, the wild animals could forage (see Exodus 23:10-13).

We were meant to be generous because the earth belongs to all of us. Its fruits and its crops were for us all to have our fill and be satisfied. And yet, food documentaries show how our greed now means chickens are grown in the dark in just six weeks. They develop out of balance, with top-heavy chests and bones that can't carry their weight so they can barely walk. We give them antibiotics until their systems are overwhelmed and they are taken out of chicken houses to be buried; in the meantime we leave the cows up to their knees in waste before sending them straight to the slaughterhouse.

Somehow we've lost touch that these animals were meant for more than just food; they were God's idea for creation, one he made and finished *before* he made man. Whether they were sparrows or jackals, he watched over them and fed them. He gave Noah specific orders and directions on how to save all the species from the flood. From Job to Isaiah, they all tell of how much the animals knew their maker and worshipped him. They tell of how much God loved them and held them in his hands. It was Jesus who that said two sparrows could be sold for a penny, but neither would drop dead without God knowing about it first (see Matthew 10:29). A sparrow—that small, bobbing bird that flits about so fast it can look like a fuzzy, brown blur. A bird without the bright red robin's chest or the awe-inspiring wingspan of an albatross gets God's attention.

* * *

Oil. The sludgy, thick liquid that is the sum of plankton crushed by rocks over eons of years has managed to take a huge spot in our lives. Somehow our lives have gone from a garden and the outdoors to a car, plane, power plant, and industries, all operated by that thick, black liquid. Our word "oil" stems from the Greek, *elaion*, or olive oil. But that isn't the oil we're thinking of. The crude oil that's refined into petroleum is a mineral that has sent us into a frenzy for access, shares, and control.

When BP's Deepwater Horizon rig exploded and caught alight in April 2010, we had seen it before. Another oil firm, Exxon, caused a massive oil slick in 1989, when their tanker Exxon Valdez hit a reef in Alaska and spilled nearly 750,000 barrels of oil into the sea. But what happened in the Gulf of Mexico was worse. It took five months before a seal could be cemented over the leaky valve. Tar balls washed up in Alabama, and pink, oily toxic water reached the Chandeleur Islands off Louisiana, a known bird retreat for breeding. And around 4.9 million barrels of oil leaked into the water, killing and maiming entire species.[18] The BP disaster offended because no one would take responsibility for what was happening. Newspapers reported it, blogs were written, officials spoke, but all we saw were men pointing their fingers at each other and birds washing up tarred.

We spend around eighty-seven minutes in our cars every day.[19] We drive to work, to the store, to the bank, to the library, to our friend's house, to the movie theatre—anywhere where we can park. Cars have become woven into our fabric. They came with windup handles at the turn of the last century and evolved into small cars, jeeps, army tanks, and hybrids. We use them because it's culture and necessary with everything being built so far apart. And we try to be careful, but we still each consume around 2.8 gallons of gas a day.

In the 1900s, we used peanut oil in our car engines,[20] but eventually we turned to fossil fuels that soon powered all of our industries. And now we have reports and oil slicks to show us how dependent we've become on mineral oils. Now we have ocean acidification and mass extinctions of marine life. Now we have fragile relationships with other countries and soaring prices to fill up our tanks. We burn through twenty-one million barrels of oil a day. Globally, we're not the only ones, but when we put twenty-one million barrels against 4.9 million barrels of oil dumped over five months, we're left to think again about the finger pointing and the shirking of roles.

When Adam and Eve were exiled from Eden, we lost that intricate connection with creation. We lost the ability to sit with wild animals without being afraid, the ability to meet God walking in the garden and strike up a conversation, the ability to be at peace with everything around us. Perhaps we are now outside Eden, wandering like Cain did, building our cities, nations, and kingdoms. Perhaps we've learned a lot of technology to show us how to get more from this earth's resources, and minerals, and animals. Perhaps we've spent too many years plundering it and calling it development.

When people move from the countryside to join the two billion living in slums around cities so they can be close to where the work is because their crops are failing in the countryside and it hasn't rained for months, our hearts should break. When hurricanes and floods rip people from roofs and off the tops of palm trees, we should mourn for them. When oil spills out and kills the very creatures God said were good at the beginning in the garden, we should grieve.

We may dispute whether climate change and global warming are real phenomena, but the bottom line still remains. The mandate was simple, and it hasn't changed, despite our wandering: "You gave them charge of everything you made, putting all things under their authority" (Psalm 8:6, NLT). Maybe the truth is we weren't placed here or given all of this authority and position merely for power's sake but to serve, love, tend, and see flourish.

Ride a bicycle

If you're able, it's a great way to stay fit while helping to reduce your carbon footprint. It also slows you down a bit and helps you look at your community from a different perspective.

You'll be surprised as to how much you haven't seen in all the years you've been living there. Or if you just moved there, you'll have more things to jot down on your "must visit" list.

Cloudy footprints

Measure your carbon footprint online and see how much greenhouse gas production your lifestyle is responsible for.

Fear not, we all do it; there is no getting around it these days. However, you can cut down on how much you're producing.

You can visit this site and see how you compare to the average person. It's a little scary, but the site also gives you tips on how to reduce your carbon footprint, which isn't as scary.

http://www.nature.org/greenliving/carboncalculator

Stay ~~green~~ informed

Don't reject scientific research on the basis of who funded it.

Keep up to date with developments in the environment, and read up on various opinions before you make up your mind.

If it comes down to it and you still can't make a decision as to who is right and who is wrong, doing good and taking care of creation should always trump the alternative.

Learn more at: http://www.naturalnews.com

Keep your pen—or get a quill and inkpot

When is the last time you used an ink pen until it actually ran out of ink? Yep, don't worry; you're not alone. They end up in our couch cushions, the washing machine, and in the top pocket of that shirt—which now has nice polka dots.

Plastic pens cannot be recycled and will join lots of other pens in landfills where they won't break down, so try to hang on to them and let them live out their short existences in a loving and caring work environment. When it's time for new ones, buy pens made from recycled plastic.

Make a plan

Take a break from work and walk around your office or work area looking for three things that could be changed to help your office become a greener workplace.

Here are a few ideas:
- Energy efficient light bulbs
- Bins for recycling paper and aluminum
- Big water coolers instead of individual bottles
- Putting the computers to sleep at night

Try putting these suggestions into a polite email and sending it to your boss. If you find a few ways to save your company some money, who knows, maybe you'll get that promotion you've been wanting.

Tofu, anyone?

Burgers, steak, lamb casserole, chili, chicken salad, pork chops—there are lots of way to cook meat.

However, it doesn't hurt to cut back a bit. The meat industry is causing some of the biggest environmental problems to date. According to peta.org, "Raising animals for food is one of the largest sources of carbon dioxide and the single largest source of both methane and nitrous oxide emissions." So cutting back on our meat intake will actually help reduce the amount of gases that are being produced.

Not to mention your heart will be happy about it. Just over 600,000 Americans die from heart disease every year.[21]

And it doesn't have to be tofu; Mexican bean salads are delicious.

Someone has too much gas

Our need for more and more fuel is one of the reasons we've had to deal with so many disasters and wars recently.

If you live in a warm climate, where you are surrounded by flat ground, and your work doesn't demand a heavy-duty vehicle, you could probably skip driving an SUV.

Mini Coopers are so much more fun, and think of the parking options . . .

"May God bless you with enough foolishness to believe that you really *can* make a difference in this world, so that you are able, with God's grace, to do what others claim cannot be done."

—ST. FRANCIS OF ASSISI[1]

Epilogue
A COMPASS, A MAP, AND HOPE

Sometimes the best part of traveling is coming home. You know it's about time to head back when you've run out of clean clothes, your neck has permanent spasms from how you craned and strained it sightseeing, and your poor mind is exhausted from trying to cram in so many images and quotes and memories. At home is your bed, your shower, clean clothes, food other than survivor snacks, and a moment's peace to rake over all you've seen and heard.

We were made in his image—every one of us. He took us from the earth, breathed up our noses, set us down, and said that we were "very good." He made us with so much creativity and diversity it's impossible to fathom there's a family tree that takes us all back to the ark or to a couple in an evergreen paradise. The connections are there—in our DNA, in our mirrored human needs, in the fact that we're all pink on the inside—but we're a family whose ties got stretched out by geography and later by language, shifting seismic plates, and interests.

Today we're left wondering how we could ever be of the same stock, how one group has enough for tomorrow so they can save for a vacation and go on big shopping trips every Saturday while another has no toilets and is hungry all the time. Some say things changed for us all because of the Fertile Crescent, a curve of land that was given that name by an archaeologist named James Henry Breasted because of its shape. It used to lie over ancient Mesopotamia, Levant, the Syrian Desert, and the Anatolian mountains. Today Iraq, Israel, Jordan, Lebanon, Syria, Turkey, and a bit of Iran sit within the Crescent.[2] The land had a moderate climate and rich soil in which grew crops successfully. Some say it's because Africa and Eurasia's plates met there and created a healthy biodiversity for plants and animals to grow. Others say the dramatically changing landscapes from plains to mountain ranges meant even more variation and so more survival.

The Fertile Crescent had the early crops that have become world staples, like emmer wheat, einkorn, barley, flax, chickpeas, peas, and lentils. It also had the domesticated animals we're familiar with: cows, goats, sheep, and pigs. The farmers back then developed levees to deal with flooding and irrigation systems for the leaner months. The farmers then worked on land in an area some say is where Eden was.

When the floods finally receded in Genesis, God promised never to allow floods to cut off all life and he promised a better life to Noah and his entire family. "Be fruitful and increase in number and fill the earth" (Genesis 9:1). Humanity was still one family at that point. It was still the patriarch and matriarch and their offspring.

Then we're in Babel and there are lot more of us, but we can still understand each other because we talk the same language. But then we build a tower, not just to showcase architectural skills but to make ourselves gods. Somehow we went from being saved in the ark and blessed by God to thinking ourselves superhuman beings—and were scattered for it.

From there the Bible focuses on Israel's story—its triumphs and failures, its victories and defeats, and its faith and unbelief, humankind's oldest struggle. Even though the Old Testament tells Israel's take on things, maybe it's actually the story of all of us—what's in our hearts, the decisions we make, and how our decisions affect the world we're in.

Now it's the modern day and we're calling conferences and writing reports, drawing graphs, and brainstorming ideas how we can close the gap between humanity. We're watching the news, reading papers, going on trips of our own, and taking cameras to find the stories and find the people and see the ones who don't make the headlines. We're trying to give them faces and names so they're not forgotten.

God is with us. His name is Immanuel, and he's with us always. We hope that because Scripture tells us so, we hope it because the earth and its beings are too fantastic and too imaginative to be a lucky collision of dust. We hope so because the human body is just about the cleverest thing we've seen. We see it in babies as they glee in amazement that their feet can move with them standing on them. We see it at the dentist's office looking at an x-ray of our upper molars and how they all have an order. We see it in the old woman who has seen her hair turn from black to silver and how the lines might have appeared on her face, but her soul remains the same.

God is with us at Christmas, when he's a baby in a manger and we're singing him carols and our versions of happy birthday. He's with us at Lent when we try to sacrifice and wait for Easter and then at Pentecost, when we remember his spirit. But it doesn't always feel like he's here. Most of the time we act like a malfunctioning, gigantic family that has too many creative ways of harming each other while he's not looking. Because sometimes it does feel like he's busy and hasn't seen the brutality and the unfathomable ways we have thought of to inflict pain and break souls.

I think of Michael, the former LRA soldier and how he was taken in the first place. He calls it the time when God was asleep. His family was hiding in the dark in the bushes around their house. They kept as still as they could and waited. The LRA was starting to move away, but then his baby sister coughed. She coughed because she was sick and there wasn't any money to buy medicine. The LRA found them all, rounded them up, began their games, and marched Michael and his brother into being child soldiers.

Sometimes we're left to wonder if God is here, why doesn't he care enough to call a time out, take away all the toys, and restore order in this chaos? But then we read the words he's kept for us in Scripture and they tell of his grief at his children, his creation falling apart like this, and it's clear he does care. We see him in flesh, hanging from a cross, bleeding his absolution, and dying as one of us to break Eden's bitter curse, and then it's lucid; he is with us.

We read about those who shield the poor and wretched, like Archbishop Oscar Romero in El Salvador and those like him who die for their involvement, or those who continue to yell themselves hoarse for justice like John in the desert, and we see he's still around in them. Some of us will hear the cries of the suffering and oppressed just as God heard Israel in Egypt. Maybe we'll be at work and read an article online, or we'll be at traffic lights and see them at the bus stop, or we'll be in a movie theatre and it'll stop being acting and become real. However it happens, the cries will come for us and they'll be too loud to ignore.

Perhaps they will be the sobs of mothers in low-income neighborhoods, who've just buried their sixteen-year old sons, or they will be in the silence of a child inhaling glue deeper than you breathe in oxygen. Maybe they will be in the farmer who wants to provide for his family and leave a business for his children, but world trade laws have taken his liberties and only allow him to float a few raw materials on the market. Or maybe they will be in the girl you never see eat because she doesn't understand how lovely she is.

Some of us will go out with others and be trained on how to answer these cries. We may save up our money, take time off work, get visas, and fly out to bustling Mumbai or Bangkok to teach children English and hold them and tell them they're important. Some of us might march on Washington or sign petitions and send letters and yell through megaphones that something isn't right here.

Others will stay behind and take the slow, steady time to get to know their neighbors and their needs and try to meet them somewhere in the middle. They'll swallow fears and insecurity and press through those differences that history has placed on us and economy has set us in, and they'll learn names and birthdays and change the relationships and prejudices in their town from the inside out.

Social justice goes beyond politics and their political parties or philosophies. It's the basic human quest to do right by others and see that they have equal access to all that's necessary. It seeks to provide the refugee and asylee with a home, despite linguistic and cultural differences. It takes time to teach someone how to drive or what those odd language idiosyncrasies mean. It gives them friendship when they've left all of theirs behind for this new future.

It feels uncomfortable with the cheapening of human life and how ownership and human beings can still be in the same sentence in our lifetime, and seeks to do something about it. Whether that's through screening documentaries or following campaigners on Twitter, it's about being involved in the conversation. It's about understanding that all human life is expensive. The boys in Mexican gang cartels that are tearing up cities like Acapulco and spilling blood are worthy. The men and women in prison for so long no one can even remember why they're there because they're not visited and no one talks to them are worthy. The people who are grossly overweight and are dying from it are worthy.

Social justice is something we can ponder, debate, analyze, and critique until kingdom come, but it's more something we have to just start doing and giving. We give it to those we meet, in the thoughts we think and choices we make. We show it by seeking that others have access to water, medicine, education, safety, and a chance to prosper. We do it by asking if our choices help or hinder them in their needs and goals.

There's no silver bullet to end injustices and fix this web of woes. These problems will not sort themselves out; nor will they wait for our despair at them to dispel. It's with God with us and through us that we'll see some things overturned. It's with him that our hearts will be a little softer and not numb to another child lost to malaria. It's by him that we'll see justice roll on like rivers this side of heaven. Justice is not only for the new heaven and earth where God will wipe away every tear from their eyes (see Revelation 21:4). Jesus tells us that he is the resurrection and the life (see John 11:25). He heals and comforts, talks boldly for those who can't be heard, and remains with them in their bleakest suffering.

But justice with God isn't just mystical metaphysical ideas; it's tangible in all of us that are still here carrying on Jesus' activities and carrying his tenderness to everyone we meet. We carry it in our passion for using the liberties we have to help those without. Perhaps it's in collectively asking retailers about the sources of their products, the labor, the conditions, the pay. Perhaps it's using our consumer power to put some pressure on these companies and see them change and clean up their habits and policies to keep us, their clients.

Sometimes the task can seem too much to bear. Sometimes it *is* too much—when the darkness is so deep and complete, it's as if we aren't making any progress and not enough of us care. Sometimes we ask, "Why should I care? I don't know them." And you ask yourself why you're trying.

But then we remember we were all made in his image; we're all human. The whole of humankind is like a body in a way, and if one part is sick or sore or hurting, we'll all feel it eventually. When there's unrest in the Middle East, we panic about oil because our cars drink so much of it every day. The price of oil goes up so we try to depend on our own resources and dig holes in the ocean's sea beds and miss the mark and turn the ocean black and kill masses of marine life, and still the prices stay high because of our demand for oil and the unrest in the Middle East.

When children are turned into soldiers for diamonds we wear on our fingers or around our necks or cobalt that is used in our phones, those raw materials never reach our hands. Their murderous sprees aren't connected to us. If we don't hear about the troubles on the news for a few short minutes before the weather, then it doesn't matter as much, because we're not giving them the guns in their fight over diamonds and cobalt.

We're the "somewhere in the middle of it all" generation. We're surviving the economic and financial crash, with high student loan debts and limited jobs, but we've also got more technology advancement in our palm-sized computer phones than ever before. We live in a world that's smaller and informed, with more medical breakthroughs from face transplants to antiretroviral drugs.

Sometimes it's hard to see, but we do have plenty, even when it doesn't look like much. When we have three different pairs of boots, eight different pairs of jeans, books bought off the Internet, the newest MP3 player and the latest smart phone, we have plenty. Others have spoken about it and perhaps it's something we still need to think about—knowing when we've got enough. Enough bags, shoes, gadgets, DVDs, downloaded music, and Apple products.

We're a consumer generation; we like to buy, and companies like to create convincing commercials that our lives will be fuller with "x." But maybe it's gone too far. Maybe now we can't stop buying. Maybe with all of our excess we could fill those empty stomachs and build homes where there are slums. Maybe with all the plenty we've been given, we've been asked to give a lot. It's a sacrifice, and sacrifice isn't attractive or fun. It takes the focus off us and floods light over someone else. It raises someone up and says your needs are more important than my wants. But sacrifice is what Jesus meant when he told us in John 15:13, "Greater love has no one than this, that he lay down his life for his friends." They might not be our friends yet. They may never be, but Jesus' sacrifice for all means we are all one without discrimination; we're all in this together.

Being just is not about punishing ourselves. You are not bad if you were born privileged, healthy, secure, and loved. The world's ills do not belong to any one person. Social justice is not about self-flagellation, for everyone is equal in his sight. It's not about guilt and blame; it's about leveling the playing field. Social justice isn't here to make us panic either. Panic only causes more madness and injuries.

Social justice is here to say we can do something now, in our time, in the mundane and in the massive. We can be what is needed simply by trying our best, in whichever place we are in, with whatever we have in our hands, imagination, or heart. Social justice is us trying to right the wrongs outside of Eden, in our wilderness. It's us telling God's story—the story that's still being told.

NOTES

Prologue

1. "Christian Pilgrims: The Road Less Traveled—About Us," Christian Pilgrims, accessed January 2, 2011, http://www.christianpilgrims.org/about.html.
2. "Letter XLVI. Paula and Eustochium to Marcella" (Jerome's letter), Christian Classics Ethereal Library, accessed January 3, 2011, http://www.ccel.org/ccel/schaff/npnf206.v.XLVI.html.
3. Ibid
4. Linda Francke, "Climbing in St. Francis' Steps," *New York Times*, December 21, 2003, http://www.nytimes.com/2003/12/21/travel/climbing-in-st-francis-steps.html.
5. *Encyclopaedia Britannica Online*, s.v. "Saint Francis of Assisi," accessed December 2, 2010, http://www.britannica.com/EBchecked/topic/216793/Saint-Francis-of-Assisi/2421/The-Franciscan-rule.
6. Desmond Tutu, *No Future Without Forgiveness* (New York: Doubleday, 1999), 34-35 and "Ubuntu and Indigenous Restorative Justice," Africa Peace and Conflict Network, April 11, 2008, www.africaworkinggroup.org/files/UbuntuBriefing3.pdf.
7. "The Ubuntu Experience (Nelson Mandela Interview)," Uploaded on November 1, 2006, http://www.youtube.com/watch?v=ODQ4WiDsEBQ.

Chapter 1

1. "A Four-fold Franciscan Blessing," All Saints Parish, accessed January 14, 2011, http://www.allsaintsbrookline.org/prayers/prayer4.html.
2. "Background," United Nations Millennium Development Goals, accessed February 15, 2011, http://www.un.org/millenniumgoals/bkgd.shtml.
3. "Waste Land: Does the Large Amount of Food Discarded in the U.S. Take a Toll on the Environment?" *Scientific American*, March 3, 2010, http://www.scientificamerican.com/article.cfm?id=earth-talk-waste-land.
4. "The Millennium Development Goals Report 2010," United Nations, accessed Februry 13, 2011, http://www.un.org/millenniumgoals/reports.shtml, 4.
5. Ibid
6. "The Guardian International Development Journalism Competition," *The Guardian*, accessed February 15, 2011, http://www.guardian.co.uk/journalism competition.
7. "Number of Nonprofit Organizations in the United States, 1999-2009," National Center for Charitable Statistics, accessed January 4, 2011, http://nccsdataweb.urban.org/PubApps/profile1.php.
8. "Our Story," Invisible Children, accessed January 30, 2011, http://www.invisiblechildren.com/our-story.
9. "Band Aid Lyrics, 'Feed the World,'" accessed February 1, 2011, http://www.lyricstime.com/band-aid-feed-the-world-lyrics.html.

10. Ryan and Christina Rado, "A Little Bit of History," June 1, 2009, Humankind Nashville, http://humankind-nashville.com/2009/06/01/welcome/.
11. *"Next Door Neighbors,"* Nashville Public Television, accessed February 1, 2011, http://www.wnpt.org/productions/nextdoorneighbors/index.html.

Chapter 2

1. Esther Akongo, interview by Erina Khanakwa (Ludwig), November 2006, Kitgum, Uganda.
2. Zaina Nalubanga, interview by Erina Khanakwa (Ludwig), October 2006, Buvunya, Uganda.
3. "Who We Are," The Fairtrade Foundation, accessed January 6, 2011, http://www.fairtrade.org.uk/what_is_fairtrade/fairtrade_foundation.aspx.
4. "The Great Cotton Stitch-Up, " The Fairtrade Foundation, accessed January 6, 2011, http://www.fairtrade.org.uk/get_involved/the_great_cotton_stitchup/the_great_cotton_stitch_up.aspx.
5. "Animation: Trade Justice, Why the World Trade Rules Need to Change," accessed January 9, 2011, http://www.youtube.com/watch?v=ldZwGDXTsmk.
6. Beverly Bell and Tory Field, "Miami Rice: The Business of Disaster in Haiti," *Yes Magazine*, December 16, 2010, http://www.yesmagazine.org/blogs/beverly-bell-in-haiti/miami-rice-the-business-of-disaster-in-haiti.
7. Ibid
8. Jason Burke, "Microfinance Guru Faces Being Removed from Bank," *The Guardian*, 21 Feb 2011, http://www.guardian.co.uk/world/2011/feb/21/muhammad-yunus-microfinance-grameen-bank-bangladesh.
9. Kiva's Home Page, accessed January 29, 2011, http://www.kiva.org/.
10. "The Basics About Debt," The Jubilee Debt Campaign, accessed January 27, 2011, http://www.jubileedebtcampaign.org.uk/?lid=98.
11. Jono, "Fairtrade vs. Fair trade: How Much Do You Care?" *Rosetta Roastery*, January 10, 2011, http://rosettaroastery.com/blog/?p=70.
12. "Should We Buy Fair Trade Coffee?", BeliefNet, accessed January 26, 2011, http://blog.beliefnet.com/jesuscreed/2008/11/should-we-buy-fair-trade-coffe.html.
13. "Dry, Hot and Deadly," Brian Leith and Dale Templar, *Human Planet: Nature's Greatest Human Stories* (London: BBC Books, 2011), 164.

Chapter 3

1. "A Four-fold Franciscan Blessing," All Saints Parish, accessed January 14, 2011, http://www.allsaintsbrookline.org/prayers/prayer4.html.
2. "Forever Diamonds…A New Japanese Tradition," Gemnation, accessed January 30, 2011, http://www.gemnation.com/base?processor=getPage&pageName=forever_diamonds_3.
3. Ibid
4. "History of Diamonds," Costellos, accessed January 31, 2011, http://www.costellos.com.au/diamonds/history.html.
5. "Diamond," Gems Brokers, accessed January 31, 2011, http://www.gemsbrokers.org/gemstone/gems_and_gemology/diamond_myths.htm.
6. Ibid
7. Ibid
8. Ibid

9. "You're Your Diamond Buying Experience," Associated Content from Yahoo!, accessed January 23, 2011, http://www.associatedcontent.com/article/8008495/enjoy_your_diamond_buying_experience.html, no longer available as of July 15, 2011.

10. Eva March Tappan, ed., *The World's Story: A History of the World in Story, Song and Art, Vol. III: Egypt, Africa, and Arabia* (Boston: Houghton Mifflin, 1914), 437-57.

11. Gardner F. Williams, M.A., "Discovery of Diamonds in Africa," History World International, accessed January 23, 2011, http://history-world.org/AFRIDIAM.htm.

12. "Sierra Leone: Charles Taylor and the Sierra Leone War," Amnesty International, Press briefing, Aug 4, 2010, http://www.amnesty.org/en/library/asset/AFR51/006/2010/en/367b7598-35bc-4e4d-8a89-f312c4bfede7/afr510062010en.html.

13. "UN Lifts Liberia Diamond Sale Ban," BBC News, April 27, 2007, http://news.bbc.co.uk/1/hi/world/africa/6602173.stm.

14. "The Forgotten War: The Sierra Leone Civil War," August 16, 2007, http://www.youtube.com/watch?v=tiqHKFMPhHw.

15. "Sierra Leone: Charles Taylor and the Sierra Leone War," Amnesty International, Press briefing, Aug 4, 2010, http://www.amnesty.org/en/library/asset/AFR51/006/2010/en/367b7598-35bc-4e4d-8a89-f312c4bfede7/afr510062010en.html.

16. "Conflict Diamonds: Sanctions and War," United Nations, accessed February 23, 2011, http://www.un.org/peace/africa/Diamond.html.

17. "Conflict Diamond Issues: The Kimberley Process," Brilliant Earth, accessed February 24, 2011, http://www.brilliantearth.com/kimberley-process/.

18. Ambrose Evans-Pritchard, "Zimbabwe's 'Blood Diamonds' Exposed by Wikileaks Cable," *The Telegraph*, December 10, 2010, http://www.telegraph.co.uk/finance/newsbysector/industry/mining/8192700/Zimbabwes-Blood-Diamonds-exposed-by-Wikileaks-cable.html.

19. "Diamonds in the Rough: Human Rights Abuses in the Marange Diamond Fields of Zimbabwe," Human Rights Watch, June 26, 2009, http://www.hrw.org/en/reports/2009/06/26/diamonds-rough-0.

20. "Conflict Diamond Issues: Blood Diamonds Fact Sheet," Brilliant Earth, accessed January 27, 2011, http://www.brilliantearth.com/Blood-Diamonds-Fact-Sheet-2010/.

21. "The Diamond Mines," International Rescue Committee, February 14, 2008, http://www.youtube.com/watch?v=p6f4oodVOo8.

22. "Conflict Diamonds," Global Witness, accessed January 24, 2011, http://www.globalwitness.org/campaigns/conflict/conflict-diamonds.

23. "Brilliant Earth Non-Profit Fund," Brilliant Earth, accessed February 2, 2011, http://www.brilliantearth.com/giving-back/ and "Namibian Diamonds," Brilliant Earth, accessed February 2, 2011, http://www.brilliantearth.com/Namibian-diamonds/.

24. "Canadian Diamonds," Brilliant Earth, accessed February 2, 2011, http://www.brilliantearth.com/canadian-diamonds/.

25. Randy Boswell, "Stunning Diamond Mined in Canada," *The Vancouver Sun*, February 15, 2011, http://www.vancouversun.com/Stunning+diamond+mined+Canada/4284427/story.html, no longer available as of July 15, 2011.

26. "The Ekati Diamond Mine: Success in Canada's North," The Empire Club of Canada, March 13, 2003, 351-71, http://speeches.empireclub.org/62754/data.
27. Kevin Maney, "Man-Made Diamonds Sparkle with Potential," *USA Today*, October 6, 2005, http://www.usatoday.com/tech/news/techinnovations/2005-10-06-man-made-diamonds_x.htm.
28. Ibid
29. "Stout Woodworks," accessed February 20, 2011, http://www.bentwoodrings.com/.
30. Arnaud Zajtman in Lubumbashi, "DR Congo's Cobalt Mountain," BBC News, September 20, 2000, http://news.bbc.co.uk/1/hi/world/africa/932798.stm.

Chapter 4

1. La Fundación Niños de Los Andes home page, accessed December 5, 2010, http://www.ninandes.org/.
2. "Life on the Streets," Let the Children Live, accessed December 5, 2010, http://letthechildrenlive.org/life-on-the-streets/.
3. "Street Children," Let the Children Live, accessed December 7, 2010, http://letthechildrenlive.org/street-children/.
4. Ibid
5. Ibid
6. "Street Children," UNICEF, The State of the World's Children 2006: Excluded and Invisible, accessed January 24, 2011, http://www.unicef.org/sowc06/profiles/street.php.
7. Ibid
8. "Photo Essay," UNICEF, The State of the World's Children 2006: Excluded and Invisible, accessed January 24, 2011, http://www.unicef.org/sowc06/photo_essay/index.html.
9. Pedro Ruz Gutierrez, "Bullets, Bloodshed and Ballots," *Orlando Sentinel*, October 31, 1999, http://articles.orlandosentinel.com/1999-10-31/news/9910290631_1_political-violence-carlos-galan-political-maneuvering.
10. "Columbia Conflict Explained," *The Guardian*, accessed December 26, 2010, http://www.guardian.co.uk/flash/0,,635714,00.html.
11. "Columbia: Government Response Improves But Still Fails to Meet Needs of Growing IDP Population," International Displacement Monitoring Centre, last updated December 10, 2010, http://www.internal-displacement.org/8025708F004CE90B/%28httpCountrySummaries%29/F7F96A823690D23AC12577F400492A06?OpenDocument&count=10000.
12. "Columbia: Government Response Improves But Still Fails to Meet Needs of Growing IDP Population," International Displacement Monitoring Centre, accessed December 27, 2010, http://www.internal-displacement.org/countries/colombia.
13. Alastair Sooke, "Circolombia: From Street Urchins to Circus Stars," *The Telegraph*, April 13, 2010, http://www.telegraph.co.uk/culture/culturecritics/7586608/Circolombia-From-street-urchins-to-circus-stars.html.
14. Ibid
15. "High As a Kai," Official Trailer, Directed by Jodi De Souza, http://vimeo.com/15163409.
16. "Orphans," UNICEF Press Centre, Updated February 6, 2009, http://www.unicef.org/media/media_45279.html.

17. "Statistics and Research: Adoption and Foster Care Statistics," U.S. Department of Health and Human Services: Administration for Children & Families, accessed January 16, 2011, http://www.acf.hhs.gov/programs/cb/stats_research/.

18. Mary Bruce, "Report: Five Children Die Each Day From Abuse or Neglect," ABC News, October 21, 2009, http://abcnews.go.com/Politics/children-die-day-abuse-neglect-us/story?id=8883519.

19. Naimah Jabali-Nash "Okla. Parents Abused Adopted Children, Fed Them Dog Food, Says Report," CBS News, February 24, 2011, http://www.cbsnews.com/8301-504083_162-20035894-504083.html and "John And Sonja Kluth, Oklahoma Couple, Accused Of Treating Children Like Dogs," Huffington Post, updated February 26, 2011, http://www.huffingtonpost.com/2011/02/25/john-sonja-kluth-oklahoma-child-abuse_n_828562.html.

20. "Facts About Adoption," Children's Rights, accessed February 22, 2011, http://www.childrensrights.org/issues-resources/adoption/facts-about-adoption/.

21. "The AFCARS Report," U.S. Department of Health and Human Services: Administration for Children and Families, accessed February 17, 2011, http://www.acf.hhs.gov/programs/cb/stats_research/afcars/tar/report17.htm.

22. Dr. Patrick W. Mason, "You Asked: Why Do Americans Adopt Children from Abroad?" America.gov Archive, October 7, 2010, http://www.america.gov/st/peopleplace-english/2010/October/20101004181832aynos8.245486e-02.html&distid=ucs.

23. "Learn About Us," Rebuilding the Wall, Inc., accessed February 16, 2011, http://www.rebuildingthewall.org/.

24. "Depression: What Is Depression?" World Health Organization, accessed February 12, 2011, http://www.who.int/mental_health/management/depression/definition/en/ and "Ranking America's Mental Health: An Analysis of Depression Across the States," Mental Health America, accessed February 13, 2011, http://www.mentalhealthamerica.net/go/state-ranking.

25. "Facts for Families: Teen Suicide," American Academy of Child and Adolescent Psychiatry, accessed February 13, 2011, http://aacap.org/page.ww?name=Teen+Suicide&section=Facts+for+Families.

26. "Learn Basic Terms and Information on a Variety of Eating Disorder Topics," National Eating Disorders Association, accessed February 12, 2011, http://www.nationaleatingdisorders.org/information-resources/general-information.php#facts-statistics.

27. "Eating Disorder Statistics: How Many People Have Eating Disorders?" Mirasol Eating Disorder Recovery Centers, February 11, 2011, http://www.mirasol.net/eating-disorders/information/eating-disorder-statistics.php.

28. Johann Hari, "A Size Zero Pill, Reality TV Celebrity Kenneth Tong and a Perfect Storm on Twitter," *London Evening Standard,* January 12, 2011, http://www.thisislondon.co.uk/lifestyle/article-23913291-a-size-zero-pill-reality-tv-celebrity-kenneth-tong-and-a-perfect-storm-on-twitter.do.

Chapter 5

1. "Martin Luther King, Jr. Quotes," Good Reads, accessed February 6, 2011, http://www.goodreads.com/author/quotes/23924.Martin_Luther_King_Jr._.

2. *Lord of War,* directed by Andrew Niccol, Lions Gate Films, 2005.

3. "Call of Duty 4: Halo Killer," accessed December 2, 2010, http://www.youtube.com/watch?v=JCDXuDA2Csg.

4. Chris Suellentrop, "War Games," *The New York Times*, September 8, 2010, http://www.nytimes.com/2010/09/12/magazine/12military-t.html.
5. Matthew Shaer, "Kill Screen," *Foreign Policy*, October 27, 2010, http://www.foreignpolicy.com/articles/2010/10/27/kill_screen?page=0,2.
6. Anup Shah, "Small Arms—They Cause 90% of Civilian Casualties," Global Issues, updated January 21, 2006, http://www.globalissues.org/article/78/small-arms-they-cause-90-of-civilian-casualties.
7. "Child Soldiers and the Child Labor Convention," Human Rights Watch, June 1, 1999, http://www.hrw.org/en/reports/1999/06/01/child-soldiers-and-child-labor-convention.
8. "Project: AK-47—Burma," Project: AK-47, accessed December 1, 2010, https://projectak47.com/projects.aspx?project=Burma.
9. "Developments in Myanmar," Office of the Special Representative of the Secretary-General for Children and Armed Conflict, accessed December 4, 2010, http://www.un.org/children/conflict/english/myanmar.html.
10. "Featured Rescue: Meet Sanan," Project AK-47 Blog, accessed December 11, 2010, http://projectak47blog.com/2011/01/10/featured-rescue-meet-sanan/.
11. "Ross Kemp on Gangs: USA," *Ross Kemp on Gangs*, Documentary Series, October 2007.
12. Ibid
13. Ibid
14. "Gangs and Guns in Washington State," KCTS9, February 4, 2011, http://kcts9.org/kcts-9-connects/gangs-and-guns-washington-state-february-4-2011.
15. "Jireh Sports Afterschool Program," Shepherd Community Center, accessed December 15, 2010, http://www.shepherdcommunity.org/ministries/youth/sports.html.
16. Tim Streett, Phone interview by Erina K. Ludwig, December 14, 2010, London, England to Indianapolis, Indiana.
17. "Armed Violence Prevention," United Nations Development Programme: Crisis Prevention and Recovery, accessed December 12, 2010, http://www.undp.org/cpr/we_do/armed_violence.shtml.
18. "Arms Without Borders: Why a Global Trade Needs Global Controls," Control Arms Campaign Report October 2006, 2, http://www.controlarms.org/indepth.php.
19. "Deadly Movements: Transportation Control in the Arms Trade Treaty," Amnesty International, July 19, 2010, 9, http://www.amnesty.org/en/library/info/ACT30/015/2010/en.
20. Ibid

Chapter 6

1. "Living with HIV: Emotional Needs and Support," Avert.org, accessed January 3, 2011, http://www.avert.org/emotional-needs-support.htm.
2. "HIV/AIDS, Overview," USAID, accessed January 4, 2011, http://www.usaid.gov/our_work/global_health/aids/.
3. "United States HIV and AIDS Statistics Summary," Avert.org, accessed January 3, 2011, http://www.avert.org/usa-statistics.htm.
4. Ibid

5. "Goal 6: Combat HIV/AIDS, Malaria and Other Diseases," United Nations Development Programme Millennium Development Goals," accessed January 2, 2011, http://www.undp.org/mdg/goal6.shtml.
6. "Mass Rape in Africa Ups HIV Spread," Health24, October 1, 2010, http://www.health24.com/news/HIV_AIDS/1-920,58691.asp.
7. "Personal Stories of Women Living with HIV—Cey, Kenya," Avert.org, accessed January 3, 2011, http://www.avert.org/living-with-hiv.htm.
8. "Living with HIV: Emotional Needs and Support," Avert.org, accessed January 3, 2011, http://www.avert.org/emotional-needs-support.htm.
9. "HIV and AIDS in Africa," Avert.org, accessed January 3, 2011, http://www.avert.org/hiv-aids-africa.htm.
10. "Water Facts," Water.org, accessed January 6, 2011, http://water.org/learn-about-the-water-crisis/facts/.
11. "HIV and AIDS in Lesotho," Avert.org, accessed January 5, 2011, http://www.avert.org/aids-lesotho.htm.
12. "Hot Issues: Water Scarcity," FAO, accessed January 7, 2011, http://www.fao.org/nr/water/issues/scarcity.html.
13. "Water Facts," Water.org, accessed January 6, 2011, http://water.org/learn-about-the-water-crisis/facts/.
14. Ibid
15. Ibid
16. Ibid
17. Ed Pilkington, "Dying for Affordable Healthcare—the Uninsured Speak," *The Guardian*, August 21, 2009, http://www.guardian.co.uk/society/2009/aug/21/healthcare-provision-us-uk.
18. "U.S. Health Care Costs," KaiserEdu.org, accessed February 12, 2011, http://www.kaiseredu.org/Issue-Modules/US-Health-Care-Costs/Background-Brief.aspx.
19. Ed Pilkington, "Dying for Affordable Healthcare—the Uninsured Speak," *The Guardian*, August 21, 2009, http://www.guardian.co.uk/society/2009/aug/21/healthcare-provision-us-uk.
20. Diane Brady and Christopher Palmeri, "The Pet Economy: Americans Spend an Astonishing $41 Billion a Year on Their Furry Friends," *Bloomberg Businessweek,* August 6, 2007, http://www.businessweek.com/magazine/content/07_32/b4045001.htm.
21. "The Universal Declaration of Rights," The United Nations, accessed February 10, 2011, http://www.un.org/en/documents/udhr/index.shtml.

Chapter 7

1. *The Weight of Glory*, New York: HarperCollins, 2001, 46. First published 1949 by Macmillan.
2. "Number of English Speakers," NumberOf.net, accessed February 24, 2011, www.numberof.net/number-of-english-speakers.
3. Over 1,000 cases in 2008 between World Relief and Catholic Charities
4. Daniel C. Martin, "Refugees and Asylees: 2009 Annual Flow Report," Office of Immigrations Statistics, April 2010, 1.
5. Ibid
6. See Chapter Two for Neineh's story
7. "Hill Tribe Citizenship Fact Sheet," International Justice Mission.

8. "The Child Sex Tourism Prevention Project: Combating Slavery in the 21st Century," World Vision, accessed January 13, 2011, http://www.worldvision.org/content.nsf/learn/globalissues-stp and "Injustice Today," International Justice Mission, accessed January 13, 2011, http://www.ijm.org/ourwork/injusticetoday.
9. The Millennium Development Goals Report 2010, United Nations, 20.
10. Ibid
11. Professor Michael Sandels on Philosophy of Justice, "What's a Fair Start?" http://www.bbc.co.uk/iplayer/, no longer available as of February 23, 2011.

Chapter 8

1. *La Vie En Rose*, directed by Olivier Dahan, Warner Bros. Pictures, 2007.
2. Rick Jervis, "Child Sex Rings Spike During Super Bowl Week," *USA Today*, February 1, 2011, http://www.usatoday.com/news/nation/2011-01-31-child-prostitution-super-bowl_N.htm, and John W. Whitehead, "Sex Trafficking: There's More to the Super Bowl Than Sports," Huffington Post, February 6, 2011, http://www.huffingtonpost.com/john-w-whitehead/sex-trafficking-super-bowl_b_816618.html.
3. http://www.callandresponse.com.
4. "UNODC on Human Trafficking and Migrant Smuggling," United Nations Office on Drugs and Crime, accessed December 18, 2010, http://www.unodc.org/unodc/en/human-trafficking/index.html.
5. "Children for Sale," *Dateline NBC*, updated January 9, 2005, http://www.msnbc.msn.com/id/4038249/ns/dateline_nbc/.
6. "Fact Sheet: Human Trafficking," U.S. Department of Health and Human Services Administration for Children & Families, accessed December 18, 2010, http://www.acf.hhs.gov/trafficking/about/fact_human.html.
7. "The Road to Traffik," Somaly Mam Foundation, uploaded on September 17, 2010, http://www.youtube.com/watch?v=d3Pc-FgEB7k&feature=player_embedded.
8. Ibid
9. "State & County QuickFacts: Atlanta (city), Georgia," U.S. Census Bureau, updated July 8, 2009, http://quickfacts.census.gov/qfd/states/13/1304000.html.
10. "Numbers" video, Teen Identity, accessed January 3, 2011, http://takeaction.teenidentity.com/index.html#/sex-trafficking/.
11. Ibid
12. "Children Are Being Sold As Sex Slaves in Atlanta, GA," Human Trafficking Atlanta, accessed January 8, 2011, http://humantraffickingatlanta.wikidot.com/.
13. *A Time to Kill*, directed by Joel Schumacher, Warner Bros. Pictures, 1996.
14. "Office to Monitor and Combat Trafficking in Persons," U.S. Department of State: Diplomacy in Action, accessed December 8, 2010, http://www.state.gov/g/tip/.
15. "Dear John Campaign," City of Atlanta Online, accessed December 9, 2010, http://www.atlantaga.gov/mayor/dearjohn_111006.aspx.
16. Phil Caulfield, "Dallas Hunts Teen Sex Rings before Super Bowl," *NY Daily News*, February 1, 2011, http://www.nydailynews.com/news/national/2011/02/01/2011-02-01_dallas_hunts_teen_sex_rings_before_super_bowl_big_game_said_to_attract_thousands.html?r=sports.
17. "Kansas to Become First Anti-Sex Traffkicking Model City in America," Exodus Cry, August 29, 2010, http://exoduscry.com/awareness/kansas-to-become-first-anti-sex-trafficking-model-city-in-america/.

18. Amb. Swanee Hunt and Lina Sidrys Nealon, "Break the Chains of Modern Slavery: End Demand," *Huffington Post*, December 2, 2008, http://www.huffingtonpost.com/ambassador-swanee-hunt-and-lina-sidrys-nealon/break-the-chains-of-moder_b_147750.html.

Chapter 9

1. Robert Lamb, "Is Global Warming Real?" Discovery News, June 8, 2010, http://news.discovery.com/earth/is-global-warming-real.html.
2. Robin McKie, "Bill McGuire: 'A Global Databank Could Warn of Natural Disasters,'" *The Guardian*, May 8, 2011, http://www.guardian.co.uk/technology/2011/may/08/earthquake-tsunami-early-warning.
3. "Haiti: The Shattered Year," *The New York Times*, accessed January 2, 2011, http://www.nytimes.com/interactive/world/americas/2010-haiti-shattered-year.html?ref=haiti#1.
4. Daniel Zwerdling and Laura Sullivan, "Katrina: What Went Wrong?" NPR.org, September 9, 2005, http://www.npr.org/templates/story/story.php?storyId=4839943.
5. Brian Williams, "Hurricane Katrina: What Went Wrong," NBC News, August 28, 2006, http://www.msnbc.msn.com/id/14559053/ns/nightly_news-after_katrina/.
6. "How Much Carbon Dioxide Do People Produce Each Year?" Curiosity.com from Discovery, accessed December 12, 2010, http://curiosity.discovery.com/question/carbon-dioxide-people-produce-year.
7. Jason J. Churchill, "Oil Consumption in North America," University of Omaha, Updated November 13, 2000, http://maps.unomaha.edu/peterson/funda/sidebar/oilconsumption.html.
8. "A Bad Climate for Development," *The Economist,* September 17, 2009, http://www.economist.com/node/14447171/.
9. Rachel Oliver, "All About: Landfills," CNN.com, October 15, 2007, http://edition.cnn.com/2007/WORLD/asiapcf/10/15/eco.about.landfills/index.html#cnnSTCText.
10. "Sustainable Materials Management: The Road Ahead," United States Environmental Protection Agency, June 2009, 2.
11. *Food, Inc.*, directed by Robert Kenner, Documentary, 2008.
12. "Rain Forest Threats," *National Geographic,* accessed January 2, 2011, http://environment.nationalgeographic.com/environment/habitats/rainforest-threats/.
13. Ibid
14. Ibid
15. *Food, Inc.* (2008), Magnolia Pictures/Participant Media and "Corn-Derived Food Ingredient I Avoid," Updated June 4, 2009, http://www.vishniac.com/ephraim/corn-bother.html.
16. Eric Schlosser, "Americans Are Obsessed with Fast Food: The Dark Side of the All-American Meal," CBS News, January 18, 2001, http://www.cbsnews.com/stories/2002/01/31/health/main326858.shtml.
17. Martiga Lohn, "E. Coli Outbreak Puts Focus on Meat Oversight," *Huffington Post*, September 3, 2010, http://www.huffingtonpost.com/2010/09/03/e-coli-outbreak-meat-oversight-usda_n_705573.html.
18. "BP Oil Spill Timeline, *The Guardian*, July 22, 2010, http://www.guardian.co.uk/environment/2010/jun/29/bp-oil-spill-timeline-deepwater-horizon.

19. Gary Langer, "Poll: Traffic in the United States," ABC News, February 13, 2005, http://abcnews.go.com/Technology/Traffic/story?id=485098&page=1.

20. Gerhard Knothe, "Historical Perspectives on Vegetable Oil-Based Diesel Fuels," The AOCS Lipid Library, Updated December 23, 2009, http://lipidlibrary.aocs.org/history/Diesel/index.htm.

21. "Deaths and Mortality," Centers for Disease Control and Prevention, Page last updated June 28, 2010, http://www.cdc.gov/nchs/fastats/deaths.htm.

Epilogue

1. "A Four-fold Franciscan Blessing," All Saints Parish, accessed January 14, 2011, http://www.allsaintsbrookline.org/prayers/prayer4.html.

2. Stefan Lovgren, "Guns, Germs and Steel: Jared Diamond on Geography as Power," National Geographic News, July 6, 2005, http://news.nationalgeographic.com/news/2005/07/0706_050706_diamond.html.

COLLEGE MINISTRY IN A POST-CHRISTIAN CULTURE
Stephen Lutz

In *College Ministry in a Post-Christian Culture,* Stephen Lutz translates missional theology to the practice of college ministry—ministry as a proactive movement that is constantly adapting to its ever-changing environment. This resource will equip college ministry staff, pastors, churches, and student leaders to minister effectively to today's college students with both depth and practical insight. Lutz walks you through the approaches needed to establish, grow and maintain a missional college ministry.

To order go to thehousestudio.com

ECONOMY OF LOVE
Creating a Community of Enough

A Resource of Relational Tithe

Video Sessions with Shane Claiborne

In this five-week study, unpack what the patterns of God's kingdom look like compared to the patterns of our world. What is the value of enough, and how do we become more like the God who is close to the poor, the hungry, the meek, and the merciful?

Economy of Love will challenge individuals to join in community, journeying together as they begin to consider a new standard of living—a personal economic threshold oriented not around the size of a monthly paycheck, but around the value of enough.

To order go to thehousestudio.com

www.ingramcontent.com/pod-product-compliance
Lightning Source LLC
LaVergne TN
LVHW051517070426
835507LV00023B/3164